We Were All In It Together

The Crew's Story of the U.S.S. Toro in World War II

Mark H. Van Auken

Kindle Direct Publishing, An Amazon.com Company
Columbia, South Carolina
Available from Amazon.com and other retail outlets

ISBN: 9781674051123

Printed in the United States of America

for Maria and Nicholas

who never knew their grandfather, but through these pages may better understand the value of freedom in our country and the costs associated with it.

CONTENTS

Acknowledgements

I would first like to thank my wife Sharon (Stanich) Van Auken, for her continued moral support, patience and understanding of this project while I spent numerous nights in my "Yeomans Shack" in the basement pecking away on her laptop computer. To Don Shreve, for his humorous and great stories, his answers to my endless questions, and the hospitality he and his wife Blanche extended to me and my brother-in-law Mark C. Smith, while visiting and interviewing him in Louisville, Kentucky. To Edward Hary Jr., for his answers to all my questions I had and the interesting stories he gave me via E-mail. To William Ruspino, who gave me a tour of the USS Drum WWII Submarine Museum in Mobile, Alabama, and showed me firsthand what life was like aboard Toro. To my brother-in-law, Mark C. Smith, a Civil Air Patrol Pilot, who has assisted me on all my personal interviews with Logsdon, Ruspino, and Shreve. To my brother-in-law, Paul G. Young, Ph.D., who assisted with formatting and publishing my manuscript. Finally, to my other Dad (Father-in-Law), Stanley Stanich, a U.S. Navy Veteran of WWII, who over the years provided me with hours of sea stories and navy life experiences. Lastly, to all the Toro crew members who gallantly served their country who are living.... "WELL DONE", or who are now deceased and are on "Eternal Patrol," .... "SAILOR REST YOUR OAR, NO TANGLED WREAKAGE WILL BE WASHED ASHORE."

Mark H. Van Auken
Indianapolis, Indiana
December 2019

Introduction

This is the naval story of my dad, Charles Willard Van Auken and the crew of the U.S.S. Toro (SS422) submarine in World War II. This story is in memory of my dad who is now on "Eternal Patrol," written by his son Mark Hammond Van Auken on December 30, 2002. It is dedicated to my two children Maria and Nicholas who never knew their grandfather in order that they may better understand the value of freedom in our country and the costs associated with it.

For almost three centuries the men in our Van Auken family have participated in the armed services during every major conflict in our country. In my direct line, Pieter Van Aken (my 7th Great Grandfather) was a soldier in the Ulster County, New York Militia in 1715. His son Petrus Van Aken (my 6th Great Grandfather), was on the muster roll with the militia in 1738 in Kingston, New York. His son Levi Van Auken (my 5th Great Grandfather), was a lieutenant in the Albany County, New York Militia from 1776 to 1781, and participated in the victory at the Battle of Saratoga. In more recent times, three other men in my family served in the U.S. Navy during World War II. In addition to my father, there is Stanley A. Stanich, my father-in-law, who was a Machinist Mate Second Class, MM2c and served on the U.S.S. 807 LST. My Uncle William "Baldy" Baldwin (married to my dad's sister), was also a Machinist Mate Second Class, MM2c who served on the U.S.S. Bass Submarine, U.S.S. Mapiro (SS376), and U.S.S. Batfish Submarine (SS310). His brother Bob was a Radio Technician Second Class, RT2c who served on the U.S.S. Macabi Submarine (SS375). My Uncle William L. Sherman (my mom's brother), was a Lt (jg), V-12 College Training Program (USNR classification) and served on the U.S.S. Panamint (AGC-13) Amphibious Force Flagship.

My purpose for compiling this story was to provide the surviving crew members and their families with a documented history of the U.S.S. Toro (SS422) submarine during World War II.

My curiosity with the U.S. Navy, the Silent Service, and submarines started when I was a college student in 1972. At that time, my father showed me his photo album of his experiences on the Toro with crew mates during the war. Twenty years later I was motivated to learn more about the Toro and its role in the war when I learned that the U.S. Submarine Veterans of World War II were holding a national convention in the Fall of 1992 in Indianapolis. By this time, my father had already passed away. Rear Admiral Eugene B. Fluckey (October 5, 1913 – June 28, 2007), USN (Ret) was present at the convention and promoting his new book *Thunder Below*, the story of the U.S.S. Barb submarine in World War II. After reading his book, I thought it would be interesting to research Toro's career at sea.

In the Spring of 1993 and for the following 10 years, I contacted 16 Toro veterans and family members to learn their own stories and memories of the Toro. In addition to recording their stories, I obtained from the National Archives in Washington D.C. the official U.S. Navy War Patrol Reports, deck logs, and action reports regarding the friendly fire on Toro by the U.S.S. Colahan Destroyer (DD 658).

One of the veterans I heard from was Donald Koll, a Gunner's Mate Second Class on Toro. He said it best when he described the closeness of the crew and officers. He said, "It was sort of a family atmosphere. We realized we were all in it together from the Captain on down to the dog."

The story takes place beginning with Toro's keel being laid in May 1944, to the commissioning in December 1944, to its decommissioning in February 1946. It is followed by a short story describing Toro's second career as a training submarine from May 1947 and ending when she was decommissioned a second time in March 1963. The format of the story follows a day-to-day schedule derived from the deck logs. The veterans' stories are inserted in their appropriate places.

I claim not to be a naval historian or author; rather, I enjoy history and good naval sea stories. My profession is banking. Putting the story together and having the opportunity to meet in person three of the veterans was an emotional and moving experience. Others that I heard from via letter, phone, or email were equally moving experiences.

It was evident that the crew had a lot of respect for Captain Jim. Some even commented that they trusted him and would go to sea today with him.

The men who are veterans of World War II are everyday heroes in our time. They are proud men that gave up part of their lives to serve their country. Those who were in the Silent Service were the "Stealth Fighters" of their time. It was a close-knit family when you were in the submarine service.

Hospitality, friendliness, and camaraderie remained a shared trait among the crew. Being the son of a submariner allowed me to open the doors into the past and hear the veterans recall their stories. They treated me as if I as one of them and that I was their friend because of my father. Don Shreve, Gunner's Mate Third Class, even began calling me "Van," my father's nickname on the Toro.

We Were All In It Together

The Crew's Story of the U.S.S. Toro in World War II

Charles W. Van Auken

1925-1981

My dad was born May 24, 1925, in Utica, New York, and he was the second child of Arthur Hammond Van Auken and Gertrude Francis (Morgan) Van Auken. On June 25, 1943, one month after his 18th birthday, he reported to the local draft board for Oneida County located in Utica. Rather than waiting to be drafted he decided to enlist in the Navy. This was the summer between his junior and senior year of high school. On his Physical Examination and Induction Report it listed his occupation as part-time auto mechanic with weekly earnings of $12 at Frank Moran's Texaco Gas Station (was a friend of the family), at the corner of Campion Road and Genesee Street New Hartford, New York. He passed his physical examination and was classified as 1-A. On August 28, 1943, he reported for duty leaving behind his family. He entered the Navy as Apprentice Seaman, class V-6, (General Service and Specialists USNR classification) U.S. Naval Reserve, S. V. This enlistment was for a period of two years or the duration of the war plus six months. On September 6, 1943, he reported for active duty at the United States Naval Training Station in Sampson, New York. Sampson was founded in 1942, trained 411,429 young men to become sailors, and sent them off to participate in the greatest conflict of modern times. Before leaving he was given a pocket size book titled The Book of Common Prayer from his grandmother Nana Morgan on September 2. She also gave him a pocket size New Testament Bible. This was a rather unique bible in that it had an armor cover to be carried in a chest pocket. Inscribed on this hard cover was "May the Lord Be with You." This was a Serviceman's Bible. The first page had a message from the White House, Washington D.C., and it read "As Commander-in-Chief, I take pleasure in commending the reading of the Bible to all who serve in the armed forces of the United States. Throughout the centuries, men of many faiths and diverse origins have found in the Sacred Book words of wisdom, counsel and inspiration. It is a fountain of strength and now as always, an aid in attaining the highest aspirations of human soul," signed by President Roosevelt.

While at Sampson Naval Training Center Dad completed his basic training. He excelled in swimming as he passed a swimming test of 50 yards. He had instruction in the use of a gas mask in the chamber. On October 27, 1943, he completed his training and advanced to the rank of F3c or Fireman Third Class. On November 10, 1943, he was transferred to Bainbridge, Maryland to the Electrician's Mate School. After completing 16 weeks of instruction, he graduated April 1, 1944, with a rating of EM3c or Third-Class Electrician's Mate.

Dad volunteered for submarine service as all submariners did. On April 4, 1944, he was transferred to the United States Submarine School in New London, Connecticut. Founded in December 1919, the Submarine School was considered one of the finest technical schools in the world. Why would Dad volunteer for sub school? There were many factors that might have played a role in his decision. He once told me when I asked him, that his dad knew someone in the Navy who served on surface ships and possibly it would be safer in a submarine. Dad's future brother-in-law and friend, William Baldwin, was a submariner. Uncle "Baldy" served on the U.S.S. Bass, the U.S.S. Mapiro, and the U.S.S. Batfish for 6 war patrols. Uncle "Baldy's" brother Bob was also a submariner on the U.S.S. Macabi for 5 war patrols.

With strict wartime censorship, the exploits of the Navy's submarine force were little known to the American public during World War II. It was only after the war ended that the heroic and daring deeds of the "Silent Service" began to surface. Dad would have known that submariners got the highest pay in the Navy. Submarine pay for the enlisted men and Warrant Officers was roughly an 80 percent boost of normal pay. The belief was held by submariners that the additional pay was awarded not for particularly hazardous assignment but because submariners were expected to know so much about their duties. Every bluejacket serving aboard a submarine possessed a higher skill in his work and a greater knowledge of his job than was generally necessary to acquire elsewhere in the Navy. He was required to know not only his own job but the jobs of those around him before he could be recognized as a qualified submariner. We also know that Dad was mechanically inclined, good with math and numbers, and had a technical mind, so this branch of the Navy would have been a good fit for him.

What Dad would not have known was the following: American submarines represented less than 2 percent of the total fleet yet for the entire war, they were responsible for more than 50 percent of the enemy wartime losses. Front-line submarines in the U.S. Atlantic and Pacific fleets took the brunt of Naval losses. One of every five U.S. subs was sunk, going down with its crew in waters too deep to be rescued. This loss of personnel was the highest for any branch of the military. The phenomenal success of the nation's submarine force exacted a terrible cost: 52 submarines and more than 3,600 men did not return and to this day, they are considered to be on "eternal patrol" for their country.

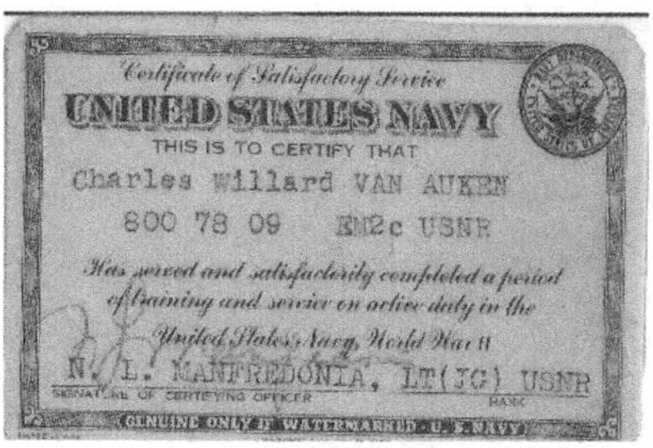

Certificate of Satisfactory Service
UNITED STATES NAVY
THIS IS TO CERTIFY THAT
Charles Willard VAN AUKEN
800 78 09 EM2c USNR
Has served and satisfactorily completed a period of training and service on active duty in the United States Navy, World War II
N. L. MANFREDONIA, LT(JG) USNR
SIGNATURE OF CERTIFYING OFFICER RANK
GENUINE ONLY IF WATERMARKED U. S. NAVY

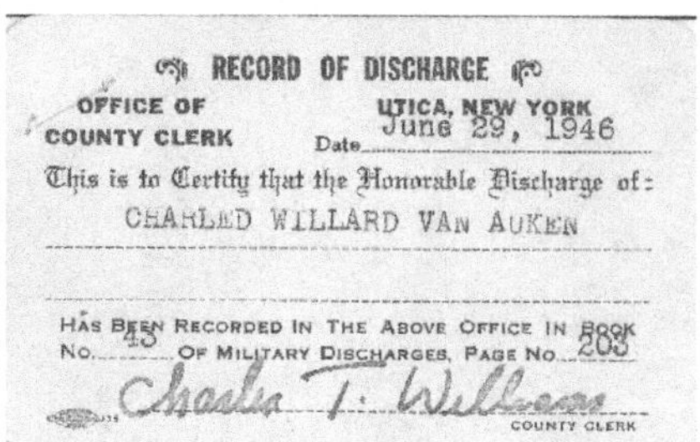

RECORD OF DISCHARGE
OFFICE OF COUNTY CLERK
UTICA, NEW YORK
Date June 29, 1946
This is to Certify that the Honorable Discharge of:
CHARLED WILLARD VAN AUKEN
HAS BEEN RECORDED IN THE ABOVE OFFICE IN BOOK No. 45 OF MILITARY DISCHARGES, PAGE NO. 203
Charles T. Williams
COUNTY CLERK

Charles W. Van Auken

Saying goodbye to the family dog,
October, 1943

With sister Peggy,
and brother-in-law
William "Baldy" Baldwin
1943, New Hartford, NY

Uncle William "Baldy" Baldwin, Aunt Peggy and "Van" at far right, at their wedding October 1945 while "Van" was on leave after Toro first docked in New York.

"Van" with his father, Arthur Van Auken

Chief Torpedoman Charles "Carl" Spritz

When Dad got to the New London Submarine School, he would have met Chief Torpedoman Charles "Carl" Spritz to complete two weeks of preliminary testing. An average of 9 out of every 107 applicants were accepted for this training. Of that select group of nine, 25% to 30% were rejected before the program began based upon tests given to determine who was physically and mentally fit for submarine duty. Spritz was from the Navy's old school. He was a former Bronx policeman, a veteran master diver and the Navy's version of a Marine Master Sergeant. He always expected impeccable grooming and regulation clothing. In addition to universal military disciplines, while on assignment, no smoking or talking was allowed. There was no standing, sitting, or walking anywhere on base. Every move was in fast time, and in the words of one of the instructors, "the way he ran that place was like a concentration camp."

Spritz's job was to break you mentally and physically any way he could. He weeded men out who could not cut it. If you failed, you were sent to Pier 92 U.S. Navy Receiving Station in New York and not the Submarine School. Don Shreve, Gunner's Mate GM3c originally from Richmond, Virginia said that Pier 92 was feared by the men as it was a real "hell hole." Shreve once saw a guy screw up to a degree and Spritz made him clean the head with his toothbrush. You either loved and respected the guy or you despised him. Spritz would blare axioms until they were fixed in the subconscious: "Around here there's only one daily prayer you'll commit it to memory: O Lord, help us to keep our big mouths shut until we know what we are talking about! There is

room for anything on a submarine-except a mistake." Learning to use all the complicated equipment is extremely difficult, as is learning to work together; so is the captain's task of welding his 75-man crew into a fighting unit. The successful submarine is one in which teamwork is perfect and only practice creates this teamwork.
Once you got through Spritz's Navy you were then sent to the Submarine School. Once you got there you were given vision tests (night vision being crucial). There were more physically demanding tests. One was the pressure test where you were put in a tiny chamber designed to simulate a submarine while enduring 55 pounds of pressure (three times that of sea level), at a depth of 100 feet. The men would plug their nose, swallow hard, and pop their ears. (In later life, I remember Dad would pop his ears like this when he and I would go swimming). Any sign of panic or undue stress led to failure. Each enlistee had to be studious and be able to commit to memory every one of the thousands of valves, gears, pipes, switches, and hatches inside the complicated submarine. Lectures and assignments kept the men up at night studying books such as Submarine Operations, Diesel Engines, Electricity, Submarine Tactical Instructions, Storage Batteries, and Torpedoes. In school laboratories, each man spent many hours tearing down and putting back together every item making up a submarine. Each man had to draw from memory accurate diagrams of the electrical, mechanical, and pneumatic systems in the submarine. Every Monday morning each man took written tests; any who failed two exams, or showed an inability to learn rapidly enough, were kicked out of the school. Every week someone else was gone. Today, many of the members of the U.S. Submarine Veterans of World War II Association who attend the National Conventions wear their submarine vests and many proudly wear a Spritz's Navy Badge. So rigorous was the selection and training process for Submarine School during the course of World War II, only 2,000 officers and 22,000 enlisted volunteers graduated from "Spritz's Navy" out of over 250,000 men who had applied for entry into the Navy's Silent Service. This rather small pool of volunteers who passed the preliminary tests and made it into the program had to meet exceedingly tough criteria. They had to possess a certain work ethic and I.Q.

Upon entering the Submarine School, Dad was examined by a battery of physicians, psychologists and senior submariners. The doctors found him healthy, emotionally stable and temperamentally capable of getting along well with other men in long periods of close confinement. He was 5'9", weighed in at 140 pounds, and had 20/20 vision. On April 11, 1944, he successfully completed the course of instruction in the use of the Momsen Lung having made escapes in the Submarine Escape Training Tank at all depths up to and including 50 feet. The tank was 18 feet in diameter and 118 feet deep and held 250,000 gallons of water that was steam-heated to a comfortable 92 degrees Fahrenheit. The course included training in continuous ascents. The Momsen lung consisted of a mouthpiece, two tubes, a clip, and a breathing bag, the last being strapped to the man's chest. The wearer held the mouthpiece in his teeth and put the clip on his nose. He then inhaled oxygen-enriched air from the lung through one tube and exhaled through the other tube. In an emergency the lung would be charged with oxygen from the submarine's high-pressure oxygen system just before he would exit the submarine. Dad passed his swimming qualification test with a grade of 3c. On July 10, 1944, he graduated from the Submarine School after completing submarine instruction. He ranked 10th out of 431 students in his class with a final mark of 3.39. He also obtained a mark of 3.26 in his battery and gyro class finishing 13th out of 107 students.

On August 7, 1944, he went to the Navy Yard in New York and attended a four-week training class in submarine battery and gyrocompass. This included training and maintenance of the Arma Mark 7 Gyrocompass, the Arma Mark 9 Auxiliary Gyrocompass and the Arma Dead Reckoning Analyzer. He also received 8 hours of training in the Battle Telephone Talker course. On September 2, 1944, Dad graduated number one in his class of 39 students. This expertise and knowledge that Dad had obtained on the gyrocompass played an important role later when Toro was enroute to Hawaii.

Sea Trials, Isle of Shoals, New Hampshire

Navy Yard, New York City

Portsmouth Navy Yard

Portsmouth Naval Yard

On September 5, 1944, Dad reported to Portsmouth, New Hampshire, Navy Yard for the Submarine Training School. He graduated October 5 and then reported to the final construction stage of Toro under C.W. Styer, Commander, Submarines Atlantic Fleet.

On October 6, he reported aboard Toro. Dad became known as "Van" to his fellow Toro shipmates, a nickname they bestowed upon him. Many of these shipmates that I contacted in person and on the phone to this day still refer to him as "Van." Van's immediate boss was John Spain, Electrician's Mate First Class EM1c, from Memphis, Tennessee. I spoke with John in March of 1998. John had entered the Navy in April 1942. Before that he had been a pre-med student at Iowa State, later changing his major to engineering. John was already an experienced submariner working his way up through the ranks from EM3c to First Class Petty Officer. He served on an old S-Boat submarine prior to being assigned to Toro.

There were three electrical gangs on the submarine. Each gang was assigned to either Main Power, Auxiliary Power, or Interior Communications. I spoke with John E. Smith CEM also in March 1998, who at the time was the Chief Electrician Mate from New Castle, Pennsylvania aboard Toro. He indicated that Van was assigned to the I.C. or Interior Communication gang. The others in his gang besides Van and Spain were James J. Kirby Jr. EM3c, from Westerly, Rhode Island, William H. Cook Jr. S1c, from North Charleston, South Carolina, and joining them later while in Hawaii was Wilhelm L. Guttormsen EM2c from Oregon City, Oregon. They were better known as Spain, Van, Kirby, Cobber, and Gus.

The Portsmouth Navy Yard launched its first ship in 1814 and later became the leading Government-owned submarine yard in the nation. It is situated on the Piscataqua River in Portsmouth, New Hampshire and still exists today. On the other side of the river is the town of Kittery, Maine. In 1943, the yard employed over 20,000 employees. It operated around the clock on a three-shift system seven days per week for the duration of the war. Toro was one of 44 submarines built in

1944 at the Portsmouth Navy Yard. It was a very busy place. While Toro was in its construction stage moored to berth 13, a barge was located next to Toro. In January 1998, I contacted Hugh S. Simcoe who was at the time an Ensign and Toro's Assistant Engineering and Electrical Officer. Simcoe was assigned a special duty by Captain James D. Grant. The mission was to take advantage of some of those 20,000 "yard birds" as they were called, who were constructing Toro, and try and take advantage of their wallets and their will power. Two slot machines were procured by Toro's crew and were located on the barge to entice these "yard birds" to gamble away some of their hard-earned paychecks. Of course, Simcoe's job also included the rigging of those machines to ensure that Toro's crew got what they deserved. The machines took nickels, dimes and quarters. Occasionally the machines would have a $50 winner. All proceeds collected under the Captain's orders were to be used for the crew's entertainment. This also meant entertainment that was not sanctioned by the Navy. Fifteen wooden cases of Old Taylor and Old Grand Dad whiskey were purchased with the proceeds in March 1945, upon arrival at Balboa, Panama Canal Zone. Van (Dad) related this to my sister Caroline (Van Auken) Borrow in 1978. This booze was hidden and stored in the safely protected watertight ammunition lockers and in the bilges (below deck) in the forward torpedo room. The ammunition lockers also served as the storage area for those mobile gambling machines which Toro would take with her when she left for war. They were used in the various ports Toro would visit.

Captain Grant was considered the "old man" at the young age of 36. The average age of the crew was 19. By this time Grant was a seasoned submarine veteran and had been on 9 war patrols and on 5 different submarines prior to being assigned to Toro. The Captain had his own reasons for the medicinal brew to be on board. He had seen extensive war-time action. Chief Pharmacist's Mate Lee M. Neidlinger who was from Omaha, Nebraska, was also a seasoned submarine veteran and known to the crew as "Doc", recommended that the crew not only have the whiskey for relaxation, but it was the best source for multi-vitamins. Don Shreve told me in April 1993, that a shot of whiskey was given to each of the crew who were takers by Doc Neidlinger twice a day. Doc would be around at 1000 and 1400 hours with his shot glass, whiskey and notebook to make his recordings of takers. Shreve felt that it helped nullify the adrenalin after a strenuous or risky maneuver while on patrol. It would be taken straight or in coffee, better known as "blackjack" or "coffee royale".

The crew also decided they needed a mascot for their new boat. So, with some of those leftover gambling proceeds the crew decided to buy a dog. Since Toro means bull, the crew decided on a Boston Bull Terrier and they would name him Toro. Toro was born August 3, 1944, at the Dodge Kennels in Marlborough, New Hampshire. Framed below deck was his pedigree chart. It showed that his owner was the U.S.S. Toro. His official rank upon entering the Navy was Mascot 2c.

Navy Dog, Who Gets Dish of Beer at Bedtime, Is Winding Up 28-Day Sick Leave Here

"MASCOT 1/C" TORO

Toro, a real Navy dog who likes his dish of beer before bedtime, is winding up a 28-day sick leave at the home of Mrs. Mary Smith, 1007 Belmont ave.

Shortly he'll be back aboard the submarine Toro, whose mascot he is. The dog, a Boston bull, [illegible] the sub when she sank [illegible] in the Pacific; he [illegible] Tokyo Bay when [illegible] came, and he un[illegible] several depth bombings with the rest of the Toro's crew.

He's got a mild case of battle fatigue from the strain of the bombings — jumps everytime there's a loud noise. But he received his sick leave to have a tumor removed from a leg at the University of Pennsylvania veterinary hospital. Mrs. Smith's nephew, Fireman 1/c Joseph Freas, a member of the Toro's crew, brought him to her home to recuperate.

The crew bought him a coat, which contains his rating "Mascot, first class," and there are three battle stars on it.

Not long after Toro returns to his ship, now at the Navy Yard here, the vessel will be decommissioned. The crew has arranged to draw lots to see who winds up with the mascot.

Whoever wins, according to Freas, Toro will get his nightly drink of beer.

TORO AND FRIENDS—"Toro," Boston terrier with rating of Mascot 1/c of the submarine Toro poses with Fireman 1/c Don Kleinman of American Fork, Utah, a member of the crew, and little Neal Riley, aged 3, of 1513 Roanoke Ave., Stuart Gardens, aboard the submarine yesterday. The sub is docked at Pier 3 of the C. & O. piers for Navy day inspection by the public.

Submarine's Terrier Mascot Likes Beer And Shore Leave

Fittingly enough the mascot of]e submarine Toro, docked here for]avy day inspection at Pier 3 of]e C. and O. piers is also named]oro. Since Toro means "bull" the]ew in deciding on a mascot de-]ded on a Boston terrier which they]ad with them for little more than]wo years.

Toro, an alert and lively little]og, is, in the words of officers and men of the sub a "true sub-mariner." He is fast on his feet when chow call sounds, gets into his place for maneuvers and does just about everything that the men do.

He's beloved of the men from the]kipper on down and he's so much]dmired by others that when he's]ken off ship he's held with a leash . . . not because he'd run away—Toro has no intention of doing that—but the submariners are afraid someone might steal him.

Chief Pharmacist's Mate Lee M. Neidlinger is authority for the statement that "Toro" likes his beer, going for the fluid in a big way. When "Toro" gets too much beer under his skin he is inclined to list a little to the starboard, Neidlinger says, but Toro's the kind of a dog who can take his beer or leave it alone.

Like all sailors and especially submariners Toro's always ready for shore leave and he can "smell" land long before any of the men aboard this submersible torpedo boat can see it. When within sight of land "Toro" starts whining and looks out over sea like a veteran sailor.

Framed below deck is his pedigree which shows that he was born Aug. 3, 1944, in the Dodge kennels and that his owner is the USS Toro.

For two successful sub patrols he is the possessor of the American-Asiatic theater ribbon.

Like a true sailor he's always ready for chow call and waits topside to go ashore on liberty when the boat docks. He has his own private lavatory in the forward torpedo room, the men say.

With 76 men and 10 officers aboard the sub Toro knows all of them and instantly picks out a strange sailor who has just been assigned to the ship. After he accepts the newcomer he knows him from then on.

While he is the object of devotion of every man aboard Toro is impartial in his friendliness. He likes every man, one as well as another, and he shows no preference when it comes to bedding down on a "sack" for the night. He picks out the handiest one and hops into it.

Toro is inclined to give the "sack's" (bed) possessor an "argument" with deep-chest rumblings when he's disturbed and has to shift his position to accomodate the sailor. He plays rough with the men but never has bitten anyone and is especially gentle with children.

The crew threw a birthday party for him the past Aug. 3 with all his favorite foods and wished him many happy returns of the day.

The mascot created a sensation when some of the boys on shore leave went into a bar in Key West, Fla., not so long ago. The bartender cast a jaundiced eye in Toro's direction but emphatic declarations from the crew that he was a seaman off the USS Toro soon convinced the barkeeper that discretion was the better part of valor. Toro got his beer and as usual wormed his way into everybody's heart. Soon he was walking along the bar, carefully avoiding glasses and not hitting a single one. As the crewmen tell it, that was quite an event for both the mascot and men.

He's already been taken "on the beach" at Newport News and yesterday he was on deck when th[visitors began piling aboard for conducted tours of the submersible. Bu[his attitude plainly indicated he wa[a seafaring man and not intereste[in landlubbers—polite but disinterested.

"What's the captain (Comdr James D. Grant of San Diego, Calif.) think of the dog?" was a question.

A sailor answered "Brother, i[anything happens to that dog I jus[don't want to be around when th[old man hears about it."

Toro the mascot, vying with Tor[the sub for interest in the nava[exhibit here, may be seen today, tomorrow and Monday, just like hi[boat.

Newspaper article from The Daily Press, Newport News, VA

U.S. Naval Training Station, Sampson, NY
Company 277
October 20, 1943

Navy Yard, Portsmouth NH
Submarine Training School Graduating Class
October 5, 1944

Launching of Toro, August 23, 1944
Portsmouth, NH

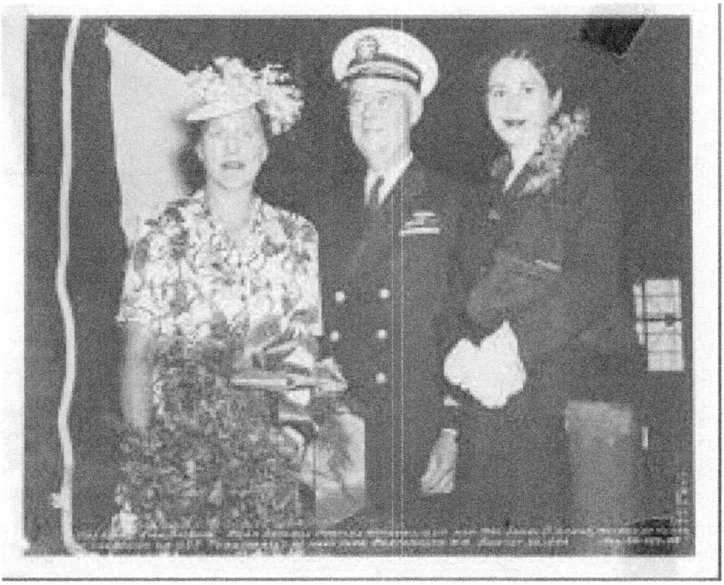

Launching of the U.S.S. Toro
August 23, 1944, Portsmouth Naval Yard
Mrs. Alan G. Kirk, Sponsor, Rear Admiral Thomas Withers
Mrs. James D. Grant, Matron of Honor

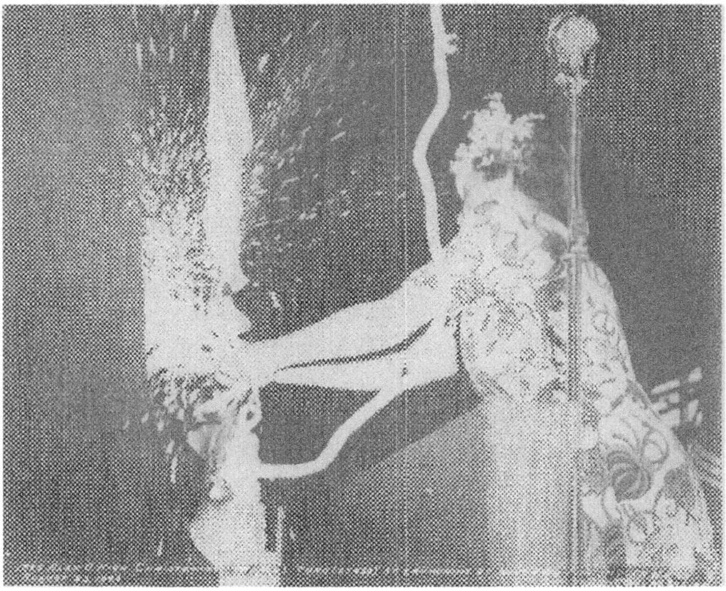

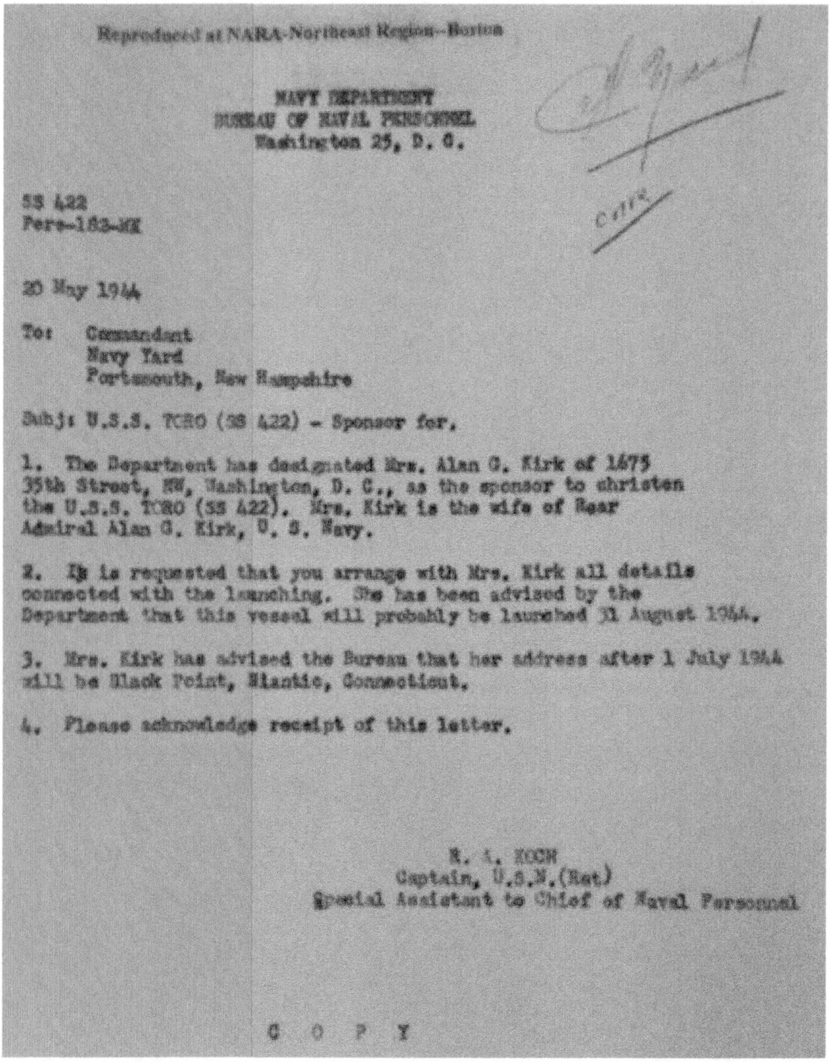

NAVY DEPARTMENT
BUREAU OF NAVAL PERSONNEL
Washington 25, D. C.

SS 422
Pers-183-MK

20 May 1944

To: Commandant
Navy Yard
Portsmouth, New Hampshire

Subj: U.S.S. TORO (SS 422) - Sponsor for.

1. The Department has designated Mrs. Alan G. Kirk of 1675 35th Street, NW, Washington, D. C., as the sponsor to christen the U.S.S. TORO (SS 422). Mrs. Kirk is the wife of Rear Admiral Alan G. Kirk, U. S. Navy.

2. It is requested that you arrange with Mrs. Kirk all details connected with the launching. She has been advised by the Department that this vessel will probably be launched 31 August 1944.

3. Mrs. Kirk has advised the Bureau that her address after 1 July 1944 will be Black Point, Niantic, Connecticut.

4. Please acknowledge receipt of this letter.

R. A. KOCH
Captain, U.S.N.(Ret)
Special Assistant to Chief of Naval Personnel

C O P Y

LAUNCHING
U.S.S.
TORO

1 of 2
LAUNCHING
U.S.S.
TORO
S.S. 422
KITTERY
AUG 23
4 PM
1944
MAINE
UNITED STATES POSTAGE
CENTS

Colors Flying At Sea

The Construction of Toro

The construction of Toro was originally planned for the Navy Yard Mare Island. According to Naval message SS381 34/L4 (728), dated 13 February 1943 from SECNAV. It read, "REMYDES 081939 of June 1942 order for construction fourteen submarines SUGAR SUGAR FOUR ONE to SUGAR SUGAR FOUR TWO FOUR inclusive reduced to six submarines SUGAR SUGAR FOUR ONE to SUGAR SUGAR FOUR ONE SIX inclusive X construction of eight submarines SUGAR SUGAR FOUR ONE SEVEN to SUGAR SUGAR FOUR TWO FOUR inclusive will be transferred to Navy Yard Portsmouth."

Toro's construction had already been progressing since May (per Navy project order dated 22 Feb 1943). The keel for the submarine was laid on May 28, 1944. Three days prior to this Captain Grant while commanding the USS Greenling SS213, received a dispatch from COMSUBPAC dated 25 May 1944 ordering him to proceed to port and take first available transportation including air and report to commander Navy Yard Portsmouth for new construction and fitting out of the USS Toro SS422 by 21 July 1944. Eighty-seven days later Toro was officially launched on August 23, 1944. "She slid down the number three way at 3:40 P.M. into the Piscataqua River in the presence of a distinguished group of visitors, officers and yard workmen. Mrs. Alan G. Kirk, wife of Rear Admiral Kirk USN now in the European theatre, was the sponsor and christened the craft by breaking a bottle of champagne across Toro's bow and stating, "I Christen Thee Toro!" Mrs. James D. Grant, wife of Commander Grant, prospective skipper of the ship, was the matron of honor. Before the ceremony, Rear Admiral Thomas Withers, Commandant of the yard, presented Mrs. Kirk with a bouquet of red roses and Mrs. Grant a corsage bouquet. Robert G. McIntyre of Eliot, toolmaker, presented Mrs. Kirk with the traditional silver bowl engraved with her name on it and an inlaid box to hold it, which was the gift of the yard workmen." Following the christening, the Navy band played the Star-Spangled Banner. The remarkable thing about Toro was the speed of her construction. Round-the-clock gangs of shipyard workers had put her together in less than 200 assembly-line days making her ready for her trials.

Meanwhile Spain was in the process of training his electrical gang right alongside Toro while she was still in her final construction stage. Graduation from the Submarine School did not complete the crew's education – far from it. The gang had to be familiar with every valve, gear, pipe, switch or hatch from Toro's bow to stern. On October 17, Van passed his night vision test qualifying him to be a night lookout. The Navy had its own way of doing things and building things. Spain and his gang had some say in where they wanted certain equipment to be located. Spain was the experienced submariner and his job was to provide further training because some of the guys like Van were brand new. He told me that at one time Van asked him, "do you like me?" Spain responded, "why, am I working you too hard?" Van responded, "no, I just didn't know." Spain's impression of Van was that he was smart, dependable, quite serious and somewhat a loner. They worked great together, and Spain realized Van's electrical and mechanical aptitude early on which he later would rely on at a very critical time enroute to Hawaii. Van spent Thanksgiving 1944 at the Submarine Barracks at Portsmouth Navy Yard with the rest of the Toro shipmates.

The Commissioning of the U.S.S. Toro (SS422)

The Commissioning Party of the U.S.S. Toro (SS422) was held Saturday evening December 2, 1944, at the Green Moor Inn, Kittery, Maine. The Officers, Chief Petty Officers, crew and mascot were treated to a dinner dance. A jitter bug dance contest was held, and music was provided by Basil Adams and his Orchestra. The menu for the night was "patrol style" with sliced turkey, baked Virginia ham, cranberry sauce, potato salad, olives, sweet mixed pickles, pretzels, potato chips, American cheese, hot rolls and butter. Night Orders were as follows: 1930 Station the Maneuvering Watch, 2000 Group Pictures, 2015 Dinner, 2200 Jitter Bug Contest, 0200 Musicians Become Tired and Go Home. Chartered bus service was provided leaving Portsmouth Square at 1930, 1945 and 2015. Leaving Green Moor at 0100, 0200 and 0230. The crew list for the Commissioning Party is at the end of this story (see p. 49).

On a brisk Friday morning at 11:30 A.M., December 8, 1944, the U.S.S. Toro was placed in full commission at the Portsmouth Navy Yard. Commander J.D. Grant inspected the USS Toro (SS422), found it in satisfactory condition and signed on behalf of the U.S. Navy and assumed the duties of commanding officer. His orders read: "I certify that Comdr. James D. Grant, USN has been ordered from the U.S. Navy Yard, Portsmouth, N.H., pursuant to secret or confidential orders of 8 December 1944 or orders which the location of ship or station involved has been omitted for reasons of security, which orders direct a permanent change of station" signed by him. Toro was the 422nd submarine built by the Navy since 1900, (including those built at all shipyards). The ceremony took place in the presence of her 76 enlisted men and 8 officers, naval personnel, yard employees and a small number of invited guests. "Naval authorities announced that the commanding officer of the new submarine craft will be Commander James D. Grant, USN, of Cleveland, Ohio, holder of the Navy Cross and Legion of Merit for services in the Pacific during the present conflict. The executive officer will be Lieutenant Commander Edward E. Conrad, USN of St. Louis, Missouri holder of the Bronze Star for accomplishments during the current war in the Pacific," according to a local newspaper. Immediately following the Toro commissioning, Rear Admiral Thomas Withers, USN commandant of the Portsmouth Navy Yard, presented awards to 15 men (who had served on other submarines before being assigned to Toro), for conspicuous and valuable service rendered against the enemy in the Pacific. Those from the Toro crew who received awards were: Lieut. Robert B. Poage, USN, Silver Star, Edwin V. Schalbert, CTM, USN, Presidential Unit Citation, David W. Snyder, CRM, USN, Presidential Unit Citation, Robert Wm. Carlson, MoMM1c, USN, Presidential Unit Citation, Allen R. Gresham, TM1c, USN Presidential Unit Citation, and Bill Rivera, St2c, USNR, Presidential Unit Citation.

Captain James Dorr Grant was born in Garland, Pennsylvania, on April 11, 1908, the son of William and Grace Leona (Horn) Grant. He attended Western Reserve University prior to his appointment to the U.S. Naval Academy in Annapolis, Maryland, which he entered on July 14, 1927. As a Midshipman, he participated in football, lacrosse, and boxing. He graduated and was commissioned Ensign on June 4, 1931.

After graduation from the Naval Academy in June 1931, he had successive service at sea in the U.S.S. Waters (DD-115), the U.S.S. Hale (DD-133) and the U.S.S. Oklahoma (BB-37). In November 1933, he reported to the Submarine Base, New London, Connecticut, for instruction in submarines, and upon his detachment in May 1934, joined the U.S.S. S-41. He remained on board that submarine, a unit of Submarine Division 10, Asiatic Fleet, until March 1937, then returned to the United States to serve in the U.S.S. S-20, operating with Submarine Division 4, from New London.

In June 1938, he returned to the Naval Academy and after a year's instruction at the Naval Postgraduate School (General Line Course), he was ordered to the Naval Air Station, Pensacola, Florida, as an instructor in navigation. In June 1940, he returned to submarine duty, fitting out the U.S.S. R-1 at the Electric Boat Company, New London Shipbuilding and Engine Works in Groton, Connecticut. He assumed command of the R-1 when she was commissioned on September 23, 1940. He was in command of that submarine in the Atlantic Area at the outbreak of World War II in December 1941.

He was detached from the R-1 in May 1942, and returned to the Submarine Base in New London, and during the remaining months of that year was assigned to Submarine Squadron 8 and the U.S.S. Grouper, which while he was attached (October through December), participated in the capture and defense of Guadalcanal in the Pacific. He commanded the U.S.S. Greenling in several war patrols in the Pacific during the period of February 1943 to June 1944, then fitted out the U.S.S. Toro (SS422) and commanded that submarine from her commissioning in December 1944, throughout the remaining period of hostilities.

Prior to joining the U.S.S. Toro, he was awarded the Navy Cross for exceptionally meritorious performance of duty in action as Commanding Officer of the U.S.S. R-1, displayed during an engagement on April 18, 1942, in which an enemy submarine was sunk. "The U.S.S. R-1 was conducting a patrol submerged when the Officer of the Deck sighted an enemy submarine on the surface. Lieutenant Grant, (nicknamed "Gunboat"), as soon as this report was made to him, immediately ordered his crew to battle stations, and pressed home a torpedo attack, executed with such splendid judgment and outstanding skill that a torpedo hit was scored and the German U-boat submarine was sunk eight minutes after it was sighted." The attack took place 300 miles northeast of Bermuda. Grant fired four (Mark 10) torpedoes. This was the only credited U-boat sinking by a U.S. submarine in the Atlantic during the war.

His Legion of Merit award was earned for "exceptionally meritorious conduct as Commanding Officer of the U.S.S. Greenling, during the ninth war patrol of that vessel in enemy Japanese-controlled waters, from March 20 to May 12, 1944. Serving with distinction from April 2-29th, Commander Grant skillfully directed his ship in photographic reconnaissance missions in the Marianas Islands area which included Tinian, Saipan and Guam. Maintaining his vessel at periscope depth and in dangerous proximity to the atolls despite the constant threat of aerial bombing from hostile shore and ship batteries, he succeeded in obtaining valuable photographic results and in avoiding enemy countermeasures."

The U.S.S. Toro: a name applied to various fish including the cowfish, the catalufa, and the cavallo, was a Tench Class, Portsmouth plan submarine. Tench Class boats were included in the last design freeze of the war. Built during 1944-1945, they were close copies of Gato/Balao boats, but with better internal layout and increased strength. About 40 tons larger in displacement, they were about a half-knot faster. Toro was considered "state-of-the-art" and one of America's most modern submarine for her time. She was a "thick skinned boat." Her specifications were as follows: she displaced on the surface 1,570 tons; submerged 2,415 tons; length 311' 8-3/4"; beam 27'3"; draft 15'5"; speed surfaced 20.25 knots, submerged 8.75 knots; cruising range 11,000 miles surfaced at 10 knots; submerged endurance, 48 hours at 2 knots; fuel capacity, 113,510 gallons; operating depth 400 feet; 8 watertight compartments plus conning tower; pressure hull plating, 35-35.7# 7/8" thick high-tensile steel; complement, 10 officers 71 enlisted; armament, ten 21'torpedo tubes, six forward, four aft, 28 torpedoes, mines, two in place of one torpedo, up to a maximum of 40, one 5'/25 deck gun aft, one 40 mm gun forward, one 20 mm gun aft, two .30 caliber and two .50 caliber machine guns, patrol endurance 75 days; propulsion; four Fairbanks-Morse diesel, opposed piston, 10 cylinder , model 38D81/8, 1600 BHP main engines, four General Electric, 1100 KW main generators, one Fairbanks-Morse, opposed piston, 7 cylinder, model 35A51/4 auxiliary engine, one 300 KW auxiliary generator, two General Electric, 2700 HP main motors, reduction gears; none, propulsion plant arrangement; diesel electric direct, two Gould 126-cell main storage batteries model OWTX49B, General Electric propulsion controls, two propellers.

The Toro insignia used on the cover of the Commissioning Party invitation shows a bull's head. One of the bull's horns has a Japanese flag hanging off it and the other horn has pierced a Japanese ship. The artist dated his work 11/14/44, and the name appears to be Moody. This matches a crewmember of Toro by the name of Steward C. Moody S1c from Silver Creek, Mississippi. Don Shreve recalled that he thought that possibly Al Capp had designed the Insignia. The insignia was on a banner sign and appeared in the pictures taken at the Commissioning Party. It was also used as a hanging sign that could be placed on the outside of the conning tower of Toro while in port. Some of the crew also had the insignia painted on the back of their foul-weather jackets. (Don Shreve and Ed Logsdon). The caption below the insignia reads: "The Bull Fish," the Toro (Ostracion Tricornis) belongs to the Trunk-fish family which inhabits warm, temperate, and tropical seas from Massachusetts to Brazil (and any sea used by the bespectacled, horse toothed yellow man). Like his namesake, the Bull, he has two horns projecting forward just above the eyes, well sharpened for piercing Jap (authentic description) hulls. His after armament consists of four pointed horns, two on either side of the tail fin, which he uses to his advantage when slapping the adversary with his tail.

Toro's internal layout starting at the bow, is the Forward Torpedo Room. This area serves as both a torpedo handling area and berthing space for up to 15 men. The forward and after torpedo rooms were preferred by the crew for sleeping quarters for the enlisted men because the rooms were not subject to through traffic and were both quieter and cooler than the main crew berthing compartment amidships (between the noisy mess deck and the hot and noisy engine rooms). Most of the bunks in the torpedo rooms were mounted in spaces between and above the stored torpedoes. Small personal crew lockers were also squeezed into the compartment. The Forward Torpedo Room had six torpedo tubes and the after room had four. When Toro would leave on war patrol, 10 tubes were each loaded with a torpedo and fourteen more would be stored on racks in the two torpedo rooms (10 forward and 4 aft) for a total of 24 torpedoes. The officer's head was a small compartment in the forward torpedo room. The Stewards Mate's job was to take care of it and the men in the forward room had to oversee its care and empty the septic tank when requested to do so according to Ed Hary TM1c.

The next compartment is the Forward Battery, also known as "Officers Country." You would enter it through the first of seven watertight doors that separate Toro's eight major hull compartments. These doors would allow the compartments to be isolated from one another in the event of damage to the submarine which might result in flooding. Toro had enough buoyancy to surface with any one compartment flooded. Under the deck were 126 Gould lead/acid battery cells, each of which were 21.5 inches by 15 inches, stood 54 inches high and weighed 1,650 lbs. Each cell would hold 48 gallons of electrolyte. These cells would provide half of the energy storage capability for running submerged (the After-Battery Compartment located below the main crew berthing compartment would have the other 126 cells). Above the Forward Battery compartment was the officer's living quarters. The officers slept two or three men to a stateroom. Captain Jim had a private room and it had a gyrocompass repeater and depth gauge that would indicate Toro's heading and depth. His room also had call buttons to signal the yeoman's shack and the pantry, and it also had a battle telephone. Some of the rooms had a fold-up sink, writing desk and chair or fold-down bench, a fan, a clock, and privacy curtains for the door. Also located in this compartment was a small pantry where the mess stewards would serve food prepared in the main galley. The tiny pantry holds a small oven, a refrigerator, a coffee maker, a sink, china cabinets and drawers, toaster and fold-down bench seat. Across the companionway is the shower for the officers. The Ward Room is also found in this compartment. It contains storage for Toro's chronometers, navigation charts, wardroom silver service, books and manuals, game equipment, record player and an RBO radio receiver. This radio was used for entertainment to hear radio broadcasts from around the world and to listen to Tokyo Rose. Connected to this radio were speakers in the two torpedo rooms and the crew's mess room. The Ward Room also housed the metal Portsmouth Navy Yard builder's plaque on the wall. The Toro crew included two stewards, whose main job was to wait on the officers, make their beds, and clean up the compartment. Meals for the officers would be prepared in the main galley and brought to the pantry for serving. All U.S. submarine officers would eat the same high-quality food as the enlisted crew. In preparation for the meals the expandable wardroom table would be covered with a white linen tablecloth. Place settings included the traditional U.S. Navy "King Neptune" pattern silverware, table silver service, and the Navy's "fouled anchor" pattern china. Officers were normally expected to dress for meals, which when in the hot tropics meant putting on shirts over their t-shirts. The "yeoman's shack" was the telephone booth-sized ship's office. Here is where the War Patrol Reports were prepared in triplicate on the manual typewriter (where much of the material for this story is derived from). The Chief's Quarters ("goat locker" to enlisted men), had bunks in this stateroom. The Chief Petty Officers ran the various departments of Toro.

The next compartment was the Control Room which was the heart of the submarine. Two large wheels were operated by the Bow Planesmen and the Stern Planesmen. They worked in tandem to control the depth of the submarine when it was submerged. The Bathythermograph was housed here which was a military secret for some time after WWII. It recorded both depth and temperature of the water just outside Toro. When thermoclines were found submarines could hide beneath them from enemy sonar pings. When Toro would be at battle stations submerged, she would run without air conditioning and the temperature sometimes would reach 130 degrees and higher. The Main Ballast Control panel (known as the Christmas Tree because of its red and green indicator lights) is also located here. Pulling the levers causes the vents at the top of the ballast tanks to open which results in water flooding the vented tanks and then causing the submarine to lose buoyancy and dive. A ladder from the Control Room leads to the Conning Tower.

Above the Control Room is the Conning Tower which is the submarines attack center. It is an 8-ft diameter, 14-ft long cylindrical chamber. It houses the Torpedo Data Computer (TDC), the search and attack periscopes, the main steering station, the firing buttons for the ten torpedo tubes, the SJ and ST radar. When Toro was at sea, the conning tower was manned by at least four men who stood watch on the sonar, radar and helm (steering station). During a submerged approach on a target the conning tower would have been manned by as many as a dozen men, including Captain Jim at the periscope. Night surface approaches would allow him to view the targets from Toro's bridge, directly above the conning tower. The conning tower of Toro was protected by armor if it was hit by an enemy shell when it was exposed on the surface. The Conning Tower hatch to the bridge was the only hatch high enough above the water to be used when Toro was at sea or underway. Below the Control Room is the Pump Room which housed the pumps and motors for shifting water in the submarine or pumping it overboard.

The Galley is behind the Control Room. All food for the entire crew, including the officers, was prepared here. Because the submarine service depended on volunteers, the food was always the highest possible quality. Shreve said that they ate like Kings. Below deck was the freezer and refrigerated food storage compartments and a storage locker for canned goods. However, this was not enough room for all the food needed to complete a 60-90-day war patrol of 3 meals per day plus the snacks for 78 men. Food was stored everywhere before Toro left port: in the shower stalls, behind the engines, even on the deck covered with boards. It was crammed everywhere there was space, and when the boat was absolutely packed, the crew was given the option of taking a few luxury items like canned peaches or canned juice if they could find a place to stow them. Space was tight, but somehow a few more cans of peaches would find a home. Working in this very small space but efficient space, the mess cooks prepared three meals a day (and continuous snacks) including all bread and other baked goods. The Galley was an all-electric kitchen. Outside the Galley was the crew's mess area. There were four tables and benches that would seat up to 24 men at a time. The watch that was going on duty (working) would eat first, then the group coming off duty would eat. When meals were not being served, this space was used as a general-purpose meeting and lounge area for the crew. The crew could listen to the radio, record player, play games or select a book to read from the boat's library in the cabinet on the forward bulkhead. Wilhelm "Bill" Guttormsen who was an Electrician's Mate EM2c, wrote me in October 2003, and said he remembered the record player in the crew's mess area and that Perry Como's "Prisoner of Love" record was played repeatedly.

The next compartment is the After-Battery Compartment which is named for the second of the two electric battery wells below the deck. This is the largest compartment aboard Toro. It houses the Galley, the mess room, and the Crew's sleeping quarters. There was a light door between the mess area and the Crew's quarters, but it was not a watertight hatch and all three spaces were in the after-battery compartment. Below the Crew's mess is the refrigerator compartment that would hold a ton of frozen meat, and the ammunition locker that doubled on some occasions as a temporary jail for Japanese prisoners if needed. This area was also home to the ice cream machine or as the sailors called it a "gedunk stand".

Aft of the Crew's mess is the Crews quarters; it is packed with 36 bunks stacked three high. The area also included the head, a washroom, showers and a washing machine. To conserve precious water, a "Navy Shower" was the common shower taken maybe once a week. One would quickly wet themselves thoroughly and then turn off the water. After soaping and scrubbing one's self, the water was turned on for a few moments to rinse away the soap. Freshwater showers were a luxury enjoyed by U.S. submarine sailors that were not available aboard most other nation's submarines during WWII. Each crew member got about one square foot of storage with their locker, plus what he could fit in his mattress cover, plus a little bag or two hung from his bunk for all his clothes and personal gear. The air in this area was usually a little better than in other places of Toro. The smell of diesel oil was masked a little by the aroma of steaming coffee, freshly baked bread and pastries, or even roast beef from the galley. From my own recollections of touring the U.S.S. Drum, the U.S.S. Silversides, and the U.S.S. Cobia World War II submarine museums, the smell of diesel oil is always present.

The next compartment is the Forward Engine Room that housed the Number One and Number Two main Fairbanks-Morse engines and the General Electric main generators. (The Fairbanks-Morse engines each drove a main generator and the auxiliary lower power engine also drove a generator). In the Diesel-Electric system used by the U.S. Navy, the engines are not mechanically connected to the propellers but only produce electric power. The sub's propellers are always driven by electric motors. Electric power for these motors can come from either the batteries (while submerged) or the diesel-driven generators when running on the surface.

The area also housed the two freshwater Badger Model X-1 distilling plants each with a 750 gallon/day capacity. The water was tested to make sure it contained no saltwater so that it could be used in the batteries. These distilling plants aboard Toro provided a limited amount of fresh water for the needs and comfort of her crew. Batteries had first priority and cooking and drinking water were second. Showers were limited to about once per week for a crewmember. Also limited was the clothes washing machine. When the order to dive Toro was given by Captain Jim, the engines were instantly shut down and all the air intakes were closed. The engine's exhausts also had to be closed otherwise water would get back into the engines. Ed Logsdon from Indianapolis was a Fireman First Class F1c in the after-engine room and said Toro dove once with the main induction valve locked open. "We took on about 15 tons of water and went down like a rock to about 400 feet really quick. But they blew everything, and we went straight back up. It didn't flood the engine room because we had our end locked. It flooded the 36-inch trunk from the conning tower back to the engine room with water." The compartment would go from roaring noise to near silence in a second. Logsdon said he wore earplugs when he worked in the engine room, but it didn't help much and to this day, he still has ringing in his ears. The diesels would be hot from hours of operation, the temperature would soar to over a hundred degrees. This heat would quickly move through the entire boat. Crew members normally wore T-shirts, shorts and sandals in extreme heat. The high humidity and extreme differences in temperature between the interior of the boat and the cold water of the deep caused condensation in the boat that got everything wet. This was not only tough on the crew, but also dangerous to the electrical equipment. The hull interior was lined with cork to insulate it. The air conditioner system reduced the humidity, but the boats were very hot and humid places to live and work. It was not only hot, but the longer the boat was submerged the worse the air would get. Captain Jim would keep Toro submerged for at least 15 consecutive hours each day on war patrol silently running (when not on the surface rendering lifeguard duty). The 78 men would be breathing oxygen and expelling carbon dioxide. On these days of long submergence, oxygen would be added to the boat by releasing air from a storage bank. It would raise the pressure a bit, but not to a problem level. One would then have to be careful to release the pressure before opening the conning tower hatch when surfacing. This would be done by cracking the hatch but keeping the latches partially engaged. Also, the low-pressure blower would be started after blowing the main ballast tanks and this would reduce the pressure within the boat while surfacing but had not yet opened the hatch. This would be a bit uncomfortable (mentally) to be on the surface even a short time without getting lookouts to the bridge.

The next compartment is the After-Engine Room that housed the Number Three and Number Four main Fairbanks-Morse engines and generators. This room housed in addition the auxiliary engine located under the platform deck between the two main engines. The Fairbanks-Morse auxiliary engine (also known as the "Dinky"), is a six hundred horsepower diesel and is connected directly to an electrical generator. When the engines are running at full speed, air entering the boat through the main induction is traveling almost at gale force.

The Maneuvering Room is where the Electrician's Mates on duty, control the source of power and the submarine's speed with a set of levers at the rear of the cubicle or "cage" and with various controls and meters on the panel above the levers. Electric power to run the motors is provided from the diesel engine driven generators while on the surface and large electrical batteries while submerged. The speed of the diesel engines is controlled from here. The levers switch the generator's output between providing power to the electric motors or to recharging the batteries or some combination. "Bill" Guttormsen's station was here and he remembers rapidly changing the levers in answer to the telegraphed orders. The two black boxes on either side of the panel are the Motor Order Telegraphs used to pass orders to the maneuvering watch crewmen such as "All Ahead, Flank." The orders are acknowledged by repeating the indicated order using the brass knob below the face on each device. Generators or batteries provide enough electricity to drive Toro at speeds up to 20.25 knots on the surface. Toro's maximum submerged speed of 8.75 knots will completely drain the batteries quickly and cause easily detected noise. The four massive electric motors, located below deck, turn two propellers through a pair of large water-cooled reduction gears.

The last compartment is the After-Torpedo Room which housed four torpedo tubes, eight torpedoes and 12 bunks for the crew. Shreve called this area of Toro, "Siberia," because it was off the beaten path being at the end of the boat. Imagine this compartment during a war patrol with 4 torpedoes on skids and 4 torpedoes in the tubes, the crew's personal lockers, the bosun's locker, and storage for spare parts and tools. Men could be found sleeping, reading, studying, writing letters, or on watch – all simultaneously, all in this small compartment, all crammed together and yet all operating independently. The signal flare ejector located on the port side in front of tubes #8 and #10, work like a miniature torpedo tube. The ejector fires flares. The hatch leading up and out of the submarine from this compartment also doubles as an emergency escape hatch. It is constructed with an inner liner that has a flange at the bottom. This flange can be unbolted from the escape trunk, then the trunk is slid down and removed, turned end for end and re-bolted to the flange of the escape trunk. The now lower end will be a few feet above the deck. If the compartment is then flooded from the sea, the liner will trap the air in the compartment and allow it to compress until it is at sea pressure. At this point the outer hatch can be opened and the crew can swim out of the compartment and their way to the surface using the Momsen Lung for breathing on the way up. They can simply allow the compressed air in their lungs to exhaust as they rise through the water, but this process is very dangerous since the lungs can be damaged if the air in the lungs is not freely released during ascent. The Momsen Lung continuously adjusts its pressure to that of the surrounding sea automatically, so simply breathing continuously while ascending assures that the pressure in the lungs will not be excessive at any time during the escape to the surface. To use the lung, it is only necessary to put it on and then fill the attached bag with oxygen from any supply cylinder. This is done while the wearer is at "pressure." That is, after the air in the compartment has been compressed until it is equal to the pressure of the sea at the depth of the compartment.

Lieutenant Commander Edward E. Conrad, the Executive Officer on Toro, was born in St. Louis, Missouri in 1914. Following his graduation from high school, he attended Saint Louis University from 1932 until 1934, the year of his entry into the U.S. Naval Academy, at Annapolis, Maryland. Receiving his commission as Ensign in June 1938, Conrad was assigned to the U.S.S. Omaha, (CL-4), where he performed the general duties assigned to junior officers, as Omaha cruised the waters of the Mediterranean for a period of two years. Transfer orders from the U.S.S. Omaha to the U.S. Naval Submarine School, New London, Connecticut, in 1940, proved to be a turning point in his career, as it marked a temporary end of his above-sea duties. In the fall of 1940, following his graduation from the U.S Naval Submarine School, after a three-month course, Conrad was ordered to the re-commissioning detail of the U.S.S. S-11, soon to rejoin the active fleet. During 1941, the first year of a two-year tour of duty aboard the S-11, he received his promotion to Lieutenant (j.g.) while serving in various departments. The second year, he assumed the position of Executive Officer of the S-11, which was stationed in Panama at the outbreak of the war. Toward the end of his cruise he was promoted to the rank of Lieutenant in June 1942. When the U.S.S. Hake (SS256) was commissioned in the fall of 1942, Conrad found himself aboard as Engineering Officer, and during the Hake's wartime patrols in the

European and Southwest Pacific areas, he again filled the berth of Executive Officer. In 1944, he was assigned to the U.S.S. Toro and served through her first war patrol which ended June 19, 1945. Conrad was then promoted to Commanding Officer of the U.S.S. Dentuda (SS335) from 1945 to 1946.

On Saturday, December 9, 1944, Toro was moored starboard side to Berth 13, U.S. Navy Yard, Portsmouth, New Hampshire, in construction status. Ships present: Various ships and units of the fleet. S.O.P.A.: COMSUBDIV 322. (Toro Deck Log). On Monday, December 11, she shifted berth starboard side to Berth 12(a). It should be noted that the time of day is given in military time using the 24-hour clock, i.e. 1630 is 4:30 P.M. Excerpts from the deck log may also include four-hour watch periods, i.e. 0-4 which means between the hours of 12:00 midnight and 4:00 A.M.

On Sunday, December 17, at 1630, the loading of ammunition commenced as follows: 96 rounds of 5"/25, 480 rounds of 40 mm., 15 boxes of 20mm, 5000 rounds of .50 caliber, 7600 rounds of .30 caliber, 1880 rounds of .45 caliber, 119 pyrotechnics, and 25 hand grenades. 1800 completed loading. On Monday, December 18, 1700 provisions were brought aboard from Supply Department, U.S. Navy Yard. On Tuesday, December 19, 1605 commenced battery charge from shore connection. 1615 commenced loading six torpedoes and at 1730 completed loading torpedoes. On Wednesday, December 20, commenced fueling ship and charging battery from dock. At 0745 secured battery charge. At 1000 completed taking aboard 65,914 gallons of fuel oil. Held quarters for muster no unauthorized absentees. On Friday, December 22, 0900 Commander C.L. Gaasterland, USN, Lieutenant Commander D.A. Lundquist, USNR, and Lieutenant H.H. Walsh, USNR from the Bureau of Ordnance reported aboard for duty in connection with Inspection and Dock Trial Board – Commenced trial board tests. At 1230 – Dock Trial Board tests and inspection completed. On Sunday, December 24, Christmas Eve, 0815 mustered crew at quarter. 1030 commenced general drills. At 1130 secured from general drills. At 1615 commenced charging air banks. 1700 commenced battery charge. At 1900 held "rig for dive drill." At 1945 secured from "rig for dive drill". At 2000 completed air charge with 2900 p.s.i. in all banks. 2350 completed battery charge. On Monday, December 25, Christmas Day, at 0745 held quarter for muster. No other activity occurred on this day. This was Van's second Christmas away from home as the year previous he was in Bainbridge, Maryland at the U.S.N.T.S. at the Electrician's Mate School.

Following her completion on Tuesday, December 26, the day after Christmas, Toro commenced her first acceptance trials off Portsmouth, New Hampshire near the Isle of Shoals area (15 miles from Portsmouth). The time was spent in training dives, drills, and ship handling exercises in cold sub-zero weather. All equipment was tested in a submerged environment as a final test of water integrity. Shreve said that Toro did not go through the full complement of tests because they did not want to be late going through the Panama Canal. Captain Jim wanted to get to the war zone as soon as possible. At 1249 the first stationary dive was made. The main ballast tanks were completely flooded, and enough water was flooded into the variable ballast tanks to destroy the remaining positive buoyancy. This type of dive was used during the builder's trials to test and inspect the hull at various submerged depths down to the final test depth, which was 400 feet. Toro could safely go to 1-1/2 times its test depth or 600 feet. William J. Ruspino Lt. (jg) from Crosby, Minnesota was the diving officer. He explained to me in February 2000, that Toro went down fast, and they had to blow the bow buoyancy tank to catch her from going too deep. Shreve said that Chief of the Boat Edwin V. Schalbert, CTM, announced on this first dive, "pressure in the boat green crew," as most of the men were new. What Schalbert should have said was, "pressure in the boat green board." Shreve remembered that Toro went down on a fourteen-degree angle and everything in the submarine that was not secured, slid across the deck including Toro the mascot.

From January 15 to January 20, 1945, Toro engaged in contact torpedo firing off Newport, Rhode Island. On January 20, when Toro arrived back at New London, at 1740, she moored in the degaussing pier at the Submarine Base. This process lasted for about ten hours while Toro's hull was being de-magnetized. The degaussing process made Toro less sensitive to magnetic mines or torpedoes in enemy waters. The next two weeks were spent training at New London, Connecticut.

On January 30, 1945, at 0730, Browning, C.M. F2c reported aboard from U.S.S. Barracuda in accordance with Commander Submarine Squadron One, Transfer Order #84-45 of 30 January 1945. Also, on this day, Van wrote a letter to his mother from New London, telling her that he saw Baldy (his friend and future brother-in-law), and that "he did not think much of his boat (U.S.S. Bass)". It was an old training submarine and was later decommissioned. He was sorry to hear in her letter to him that Nana (his grandmother), was sick and not doing well. Van also told his mother that he was trying to get 48 hours to come home. Otherwise, he said, "don't plan on seeing me again for quite some time." From January 30, until February 2, 1945, Toro was in the Marine Railway, U.S. Submarine Base, in New London, Connecticut. The Marine Railway used a locomotive engine to pull Toro out of the water and was used to inspect, clean and repair the exposed hull of the submarine. A nine-inch crack in the main pressure hull near the 24 inch forward engine room intake valve was discovered and three master welders worked all night in zero degree weather applying the hard patch to the pre-heated hull while the crew stayed at their fire stations as a precaution. William "Bill" Bruckel was the Communications Officer. He said that Toro made a practice dive in the Long Island Sound to a depth of 150 feet with the sonar heads rigged out. Toro touched bottom but only damaged the sonar gear. Dry dock repairs were essential before Toro headed to the Pacific. Bruckel felt this was an intended act by Grant so that he could delay leaving while his 5th daughter was born in New London. On February 2, at 1155 Toro commenced taking on fuel. At 1200 the battery charge commenced and at 1400 commenced taking on 24 Mark 14-3a torpedoes. At 1800 completed taking on fuel oil. Received taking on 57,930 gallons. On February 3, Edward M. Hary, Torpedoman's Mate First Class TM1c, from Bryan, Texas reported aboard Toro for duty. He was to replace the torpedo man in charge of the forward torpedo room and was informed that Toro was sailing for the South Pacific in two days. With such short notice, he had with him his wife, his 5-month-old daughter, a car, and a house full of furniture, all to send home to Texas before he left. He was originally assigned to the U.S.S. Plunger, but his orders changed at the last minute. Bill Bruckel told me in July 2003, (at the age of 85), that Captain Grant was asked what kind of food he wanted to take on board by the Chief Commissary Officer at New London. Because of Captain Jim's record and seniority, he was able to request whatever he wanted to take to sea aboard Toro. So, he ordered lots of Filet Mignon steak and some "medicinal liquor." As Communications Officer, Bill said he was always the last to get on Toro and the first to get ashore with the skipper because of his reports he had to complete or submit. One time when he was the last to get on board, he remembered the guys saying to him "Bruckel your wife just had another baby." Bruckel was a college jock who had played football before entering the Navy. He did not smoke or drink. Grant was kind of a "bully" as he put it. Grant himself liked a drink from time to time and maybe he held that against him. Bruckel observed how Grant treated Ruspino with more respect. Ruspino would stand up to Grant. Bruckel found that this worked with him. Grant one-time surprised Bruckel by pouring a bucket of ice water down the conning tower hatch onto Bruckel's back who was in the control room at his station just to get a reaction.

On February 5, at 1000, Lehnemann, L.J., TM3c reported aboard for duty. At 1300, Rear Admiral C.W. Styer (Commander Submarines Atlantic Fleet), and staff came aboard on departure inspection. At 1400 Rear Admiral C.W. Styer and staff left ship. At 1645 the maneuvering watch was stationed and preparations for getting underway were made in accordance with ComSubLant Order 80-45. At 1707, Toro was underway "unescorted" per orders on various courses and speeds conforming to the Thames River channel. At 1801 set course 194 T and pgc, (194 true compass degrees and per gyro compass) and standard speed (12 knots). During the day Toro while surfaced, commenced zigzagging in accordance with standard zig-zag plan #40 as she headed southwest along the East Coast. Toro was equipped with an Arma Course Clock that was programmed to either a zig plan or a constant helm plan. The helmsman stayed on the mark southwest or 194 degrees, yet Toro wandered back and forth across this course on a timed sequence. Toro's navigator would know precisely what actual speed was being made along the base course line of advance, dependent upon the zig plan input. This was a defensive measure against possible German U-Boats that might have been lurking off the coast. The operational orders warned, "enemy submarines may be expected at any time in the Western Atlantic Area and within the Sea Frontiers, and mines planted by enemy submarines have been discovered in coastal waters."

On February 6, Toro followed the East River Channel heading south into the greater New York area. When Toro finally left the New York harbor area she was in company with escort P.C. 1175 the rest of the trip to Key West. In addition, Toro's orders stated "friendly aircraft patrols may be encountered at any time along the route prescribed. Friendly submarines enroute have been fired on by friendly merchantmen and should be given wide berth not approaching closer than six miles if possible". Toro flew only the U.S. flag to identify her as friendly but her "422" hull number had been painted over. Operational orders would always specify where to obtain fuel and provisions and in this case, it specified "fuel and provision to capacity at Submarine Base, New London, Connecticut and at Naval Station, Balboa, Canal Zone."

In 1997, two wreck divers by the names of John Chatterton and Richie Kohler identified the sunken remains of the WWII German U-Boat U-869 off the coast of New Jersey not far from the very route Toro would be following. On December 8, 1945 U-869 left Norway on her first patrol. Ironically this was the same day as Toro's commissioning. U-869 was headed to naval grid CA53 located about 110 miles southeast of New York City. On January 17, 1945, the Allies picked up coded messages sent from Germany to U-869. (The German code had already been deciphered by this time in the war and the enigma encoding machine had already been captured from U-505). American intelligence was then informed and responded with a hunter-killer group to try and pickup and destroy U-869. Toro's operational order dated January 31, warned of this very type of U-Boat activity that she may encounter along the way. Then at the beginning of February, U-869 was ordered to patrol at a point about 70 miles southeast of the New York approaches. Now being in American waters, U-869 would have been bearing down on whatever enemy targets she could find. Ironically, U-869 like Toro was on her very first war patrol and neither sub had ever fired a torpedo at an enemy ship before. On or around this date it is believed that U-869 must have spotted an enemy ship. It is believed that she fired her first torpedo and that it turned out to be a fatal circle-runner that came back around and sank her. One will never know if U-869 saw Toro on the surface zig-zagging enroute to Key West in the crosshairs of her periscope and the torpedo she fired was intended for Toro. Possibly that is why Toro's orders had changed and she picked up for added protection escort P.C. 1175 (Navy submarine chaser) in New York to be with her until she got to Key West.

On February 10, Toro safely completed without incident her longest trip to date from New London to Key West. At 0954, she moored starboard side to DE 182, Pier A, N.O.B., at Key West, Florida. Ships present, various units of U.S. Fleet. S.O.P.A., and reported to the officer in charge of the Fleet Sound School. (S.O.P.A. means the "senior officer present afloat").

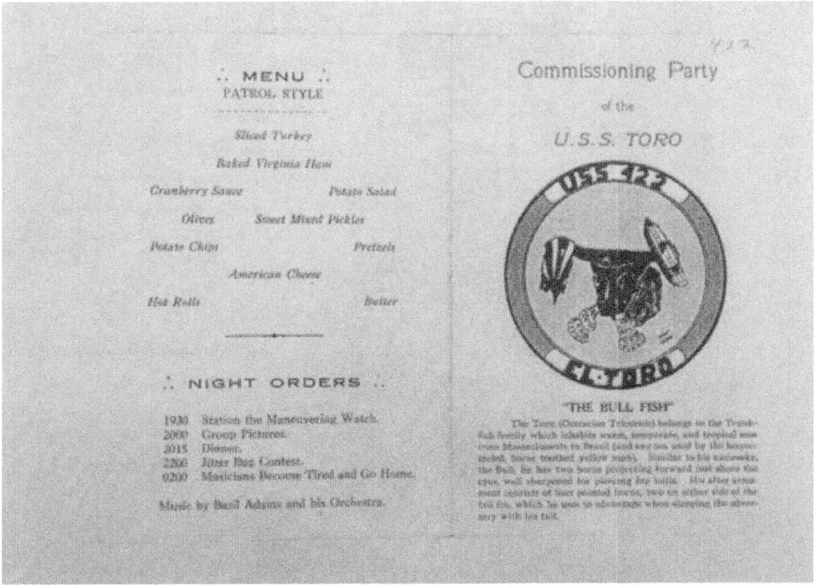

∴ MENU ∴
PATROL STYLE

Sliced Turkey

Baked Virginia Ham

Cranberry Sauce *Potato Salad*

Olives *Sweet Mixed Pickles*

Potato Chips *Pretzels*

American Cheese

Hot Rolls *Butter*

∴ NIGHT ORDERS ∴

1930 Station the Maneuvering Watch.
2000 Group Pictures.
2015 Dinner.
2200 Jitter Bug Contest.
0200 Musicians Become Tired and Go Home.

Music by Basil Adams and his Orchestra.

Commissioning Party

of the

U.S.S. TORO

"THE BULL FISH"

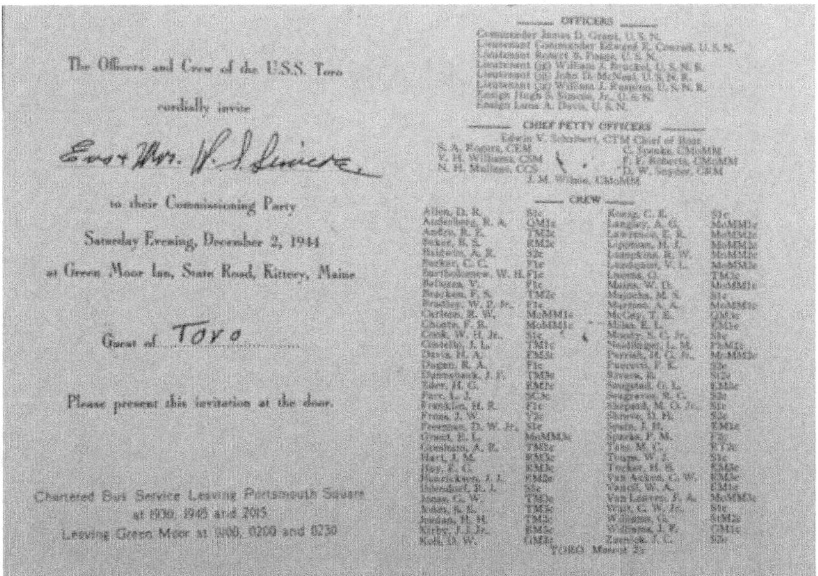

The Officers and Crew of the U.S.S. Toro

cordially invite

Ens + Mrs. V. I. Sinicke

to their Commissioning Party

Saturday Evening, December 2, 1944

at Green Moor Inn, State Road, Kittery, Maine

Guest of Toro

Please present this invitation at the door.

Chartered Bus Service Leaving Portsmouth Square
at 1930, 1945 and 2015
Leaving Green Moor at 0100, 0200 and 0230

OFFICERS

CHIEF PETTY OFFICERS

CREW

U.S.S. TORO

U.S.S. TORO

Commissioning Party 12/2/44

U.S.S. TORO

"THE BULL FISH"

The Toro (Ostracion Tricornis) belongs to the Trunk-fish family which inhabits warm, temperate, and tropical seas from Massachusetts to Brazil (and any sea used by the bespectacled, horse toothed yellow man). Similar to his namesake, the Bull, he has two horns projecting forward just above the eyes, well sharpened for piercing Jap hulls. His after armament consists of four pointed horns, two on either side of the tail fin, which he uses to advantage when slapping the adversary with his tail.

Key West

During the next two weeks while operating out of Key West, Toro rendered services to the Fleet Sonar School per operational orders. While not on duty, the crew of Toro enjoyed their time in the warm southern Florida sun and enjoyed themselves. It was a far cry from the bitter cold New England winter they had left behind five days before. In May of 1993, I contacted Roy A. Anderberg who served as Quartermaster QM1c from Boston, Massachusetts. He took many pictures of the crew while in Key West. As he described it, "I would conceal this tiny Kodak 828 camera in my watch pocket of my white uniform, and I would pull the white jacket down so no one could see I had a camera." There were beach pictures taken of guys in their swimming suits, which included Smith CEM, Van EM3c, Cook FC3c, Konig F1c, Zarnic S1c, Anderberg QM1c, Parry RT2c, and Toups S1c. There were pictures taken of guys in bathing suits climbing palm trees. (These pictures were in my father's Toro photo album he showed me). There were also good times going on in the bars on Duval Street. Anderberg said that he was first introduced to Rum and Cokes while on liberty by Joseph W. Freas Yeoman Y2c from Cape May, New Jersey. It was known that Freas, after having a few drinks and feeling good, would come under the watchful eye of the Shore Patrol. Shreve said he was the fastest running guy he could remember. Freas would kick off his shoes and take off running away from the Shore Patrol in his stocking feet down the street or alley, never getting caught. Even Toro the mascot enjoyed his shore leave. As it was described in an article written about Toro (Daily Press newspaper in Newport News, Va. October 27, 1945), at the end of the war, "Toro created a sensation when some of the boys took him to a bar. The bartender cast a jaundiced eye in Toro's direction but emphatic declarations from the crew that he was a seaman off the U.S.S. Toro soon convinced the barkeeper that discretion was the better part of valor. Toro got his beer and as usual wormed his way into everybody's heart. Soon he was walking along the bar, carefully avoiding glasses and not hitting a single one. As the crewmen tell it, that was quite an event for both the mascot and men. What's the Captain to think of the dog? A sailor answered, brother, if anything happens to that dog I just don't want to be around when the old man hears about it."

On February 26, 1945, while still in Key West, moored as before. 0800, daily inspection of magazine and smokeless powder samples. Conditions normal. Mustered crew at quarters: no absentees. 1035 broke Rear-Admiral C.W. Styers, ComSubLant's flag. Ed Hary said that this meant that the flag was hoisted aft of the periscope rigging when he was present. On the next day, 0645 secured battery charge. 0730 hauled down flag of Rear Admiral C.W. Styers, ComSubLant, (he left ship), and broke commission pennant. On February 28, 12-16 Watch: Moored as before. 1417 went to fire quarters for overheated panel in maneuvering room. 1419 secured from fire quarters. 1420 tugs Rufus Goldberg and YMT 231 made fast her lines alongside. Lt. (jg) J.B. Hallitt, Lt. Freebuger and Chief Boatswain Dugan came aboard. 1431 underway in tow. 1445 Lt. (jg) J.B. Hallitt, Lt. Freebuger and Chief Boatswain Dugan left the ship. Tugs cast off. Underway on various courses and speeds conforming to the channel. 1513 passed Buoy 1B to starboard, distance 50 yards. Set course 180 T and pgc, speed standard. 1525 joined U.S.S. Bumper (SS 333), and escort PC 1145 in accordance with ComSubsLant operation order 80-45, dated January 31, 1945, enroute for the Panama Canal. At 1610, Lt(jg) W.J. Ruspino, lacerated back of left hand about 2" in length and ¼ "deep. Six stiches were taken by the Pharmacist Mate (Doc), and sulfadiazine drugs were administered. Doc also treated Shreve who had and an ingrown big toenail. He removed the nail and left the toe quite sore according to Shreve. When Toro pulled into the Panama Canal area, Shreve said, "in order to go ashore on liberty, I cut the top of my shoe off to eliminate the pressure. The Shore Patrol tried to send me back to the boat because I was out of regulation uniform. I told them to go to hell, and strangely enough, they let me go."

On March 3, underway in accordance with ComSubLant operation order #80-45, dated 31 January 1945, in company with U.S.S. Bumper (SS333), on base course 176 T and pgc., standard speed (17 knots). At 1248 underway as before and slowed to one-third speed and commenced to maneuvering on various courses in order to put a loose deck line back in locker. At 1250 secured line and resumed zigzag at standard speed.

On March 4, 1945, 0707 passed East Breakwater Light abeam to port 100 yards, entered Christobol Harbor Panama Canal Zone. 0726 Pilot Mr. John W. Anderson and Lt. B.C. Cooley, USNR, came aboard. 0734 lying to inside the harbor. At 0750 underway on main engines. 0800 made daily inspection of magazine and smokeless powder samples. The smokeless powder was used as a propellant for the 5" deck gun and was in silk bags. The bags were stowed in magazines in airtight metal tanks. Conditions normal. 0855 entering Gatun Lock. At 0950 transit of Gatun Lock was completed. Underway at various courses and speeds through canal. 1005 commenced battery charge. 1233 commenced transit of Pedro Miguel Locks. 1303 completed transit of lock. Underway through canal. 1312 commenced transit of Miraflores Lock. 1343 completed transit of lock. Underway in transit of canal. 1440 moored port side of U.S.S. Bumper, Berth C, N.O.B., Balboa, Canal Zone on the Pacific side. 1445, pilot John W. Anderson and Lt. B.C. Cooley, left ship.

Shreve related a story about C.W. Wait Jr., Seaman First Class S1c, who was nicknamed "Two Beers." It was common knowledge that when "Two Beers" had two beers, he would become squirrely eyed and steal gas caps for whatever reason. The Panama Canal has an 18-foot tide. Toro was tied up at the pier and Shreve had the topside watch. "Two Beers" had a four-hour pass to go ashore on liberty and when he left the pier Toro was even with the pier. When ole "Two Beers" returned later from his 4-hour liberty, he ran down the gangplank to Toro. Meanwhile, the tide had gone out while he was away, and Toro was 18 feet below the pier. So, the gangplank was on a steep down angle. A cruiser ship was moored on the other side of the pier and a bunch of sailors happened to be watching "Two Beers" running down the gangplank returning to board Toro. Shreve noticed that his blue jumper top was bulging, and when he hit the deck of Toro, a large number of stolen gas caps fell out from under his jumper top. When "Two Beers" ran over to the after-battery hatch to enter Toro, Shreve attempted to help him down the ladder. Instead "Two Beers" fell through the hatch. Meanwhile, the audience watching the whole time on the cruiser ship were laughing the entire time. They wondered if he was okay. When Shreve looked down the hatch, he saw that Ole "Two

Beers" had landed on his two feet. Shreve yelled over to the audience "he's okay."

For the next eleven days Toro underwent intensive training in the Canal Zone under Commander Submarine Squadron Three. This training included practice torpedo approaches, firing 22 practice torpedoes, conducting sound tests at various speeds, and conducting radar radiation periscope tests with USS Bulmer escort destroyer. On March 9, at 1555 the USS Bulmer dropped two practice depth charges on Toro to simulate an attack. Later that day at 1902 Toro conducted night bombardment exercises where they fired 14 rounds of 5" ammunition. On March 10, 1430 battle surfaced on course 000T and pgc. Expended five rounds of five-inch ammunition at target towed by U.S.S. Mallard. 1435 dived on course 000T and pgc. 1437 battle stations surface set. 1440 battle surfaced on course 000T and pgc, fired at towed target with 5" deck gun, 40mm, 20mm, and .30 cal. machine guns. Expended 10 rounds of five-inch ammunition, 120 rounds of 40 mm, 40 rounds of 20mm, and 750 rounds of .30 cal. ammunition. 1510 secured from battle stations surface. On March 13, Toro began taking on provisions, ammunition and fuel. She took on from the Navy ammunition depot, #121: 10 rounds 5"/25 H.C. projectiles; 160 rounds 40 mm A.A. ammunition. On March 14, she took on twenty MK 14, 3-A torpedoes, 7992 gallons of fuel, and loaded aboard five rounds of 5" common ammunition. On March 15, 1129 Toro was underway in accordance with ComSubRon 3 operation order 141519 dated March 14, 1945. After exiting the army's-controlled minefield that guarded the approach to Balboa Harbor, Toro set a westward course for Hawaii in company with U.S.S. Bumper (SS333).

During the next fifteen days Toro and Bumper while enroute to Pearl, conducted training exercises. They made practice approaches while manning battle stations surface with each other. They also conducted practice torpedo approaches on each other. They always traveled on the surface and when not training they would resume their zig-zag plan while traveling at standard speed (14 knots). On March 18, 0051 upon request of U.S.S. Bumper, Toro stopped all engines. At 0126 Neidlinger CPhM was taken over to U.S.S. Bumper in rubber lifeboat to assist in care of patient. At 0150 the rubber boat and crew returned. At 0830 Neidlinger returned aboard Toro. U.S.S. Bumper proceeded under separate orders. On March 28, 1140 Toro made contact with U.S.S. Bumper which joined formation. They remained in company with each other and resumed their training which included practice approaches and quick dives.

Shreve told me about his scariest moment aboard Toro was when he was serving as a starboard forward lookout topside in the periscope shears. They were conducting one of the many diving training exercises. When the diving alarm sounded, everyone topside cleared the bridge. Normally there were three lookouts assigned overlapping sectors. As a starboard lookout your job was to cover the sector between 350 degrees – 130 degrees (relative) and look for enemy vessels or planes and make all reports of sightings immediately to the OOD (Officer of the Deck). Shreve's diving station (in accordance with the Watch, Quarter, and Station Bill) was to man the bow planes in the control room. Shreve put the bow planes in gear for FULL DIVE. The bow planes started rigging out and Toro began to dive. Ruspino who was the diving officer, ordered the prescribed depth and at the appropriate time ordered the bow planes up to level off the dive. However, when Shreve tried to do as ordered the bow planes were jammed in FULL DIVE. He quickly grabbed the T-handle to move it out and down in order to use the wheel manually. It did not engage. Toro continued to dive. In fear, Shreve started to get up out of his seat for a second, stopped in his tracks and said to himself, "where, in the Hell, am I going," and then quickly turned back and sat down again. He quickly grabbed the T-handle and threw it down and up. The hydraulics kicked in and the wheel responded. The bow planes moved up to level off Toro to the ordered depth. Later, when Shreve was walking through the officer's quarters, he ran into Mr. Ruspino who asked him "what happened out there?" Shreve responded, "the bow planes jammed in FULL DIVE and I lost it. I was getting ready to take off and then went back and sat down. Will that go against my record?" Mr. Ruspino responded, "no, but if you wouldn't have gone back it would have gone against you." Shreve wrote a poem about the Bowplanesman:

The Bowplanesman's Ballad

The poor bowplanesman lay dying,
His life was fast ebbing away.
To his shipmates all gathered around him,
These last dying words he did say.
"The ordered depth was four hundred,
Four hundred I reached and did stay-
But now that the danger is over,
Let's surface and get underway."

He moved in his place very weakly
And beckoned to the chief of the watch.
I moved up and listened quite closely,
But these words were all that I got.
"Take the depth gauge out of my stomach;
Take the dive bubble out of my spine;
Put the bowplanes back into power;
Put four engines back on the line."

Now the bowplanesman was a gunner,
His rating was gunner's third class.
As he felt himself going under,
This dying request he did ask.
"If we ever get to the surface,
And my life here on Earth it is done,
Put my 'U' tool under my shoulder-
And lay me out under my gun."

"And as you are sliding me over,
Down to the bottom of the sea,
Oh, load it and fire a shot o'er;
If it jams throw it in after me.
And as I'm sinking quite quickly,
Headed for the bottom pell-mell,
And I see that jammed 'Forty' beside me,
Don't worry, I'll clear it in Hell!!

He smiled a smile of real calmness,

His hands fell back on his chest.
His life he had lived in completeness,
And now he has gone to his rest:

Shreve remembered that Ruspino had a record that he played on the record player in the officer's quarter incessantly. It was called Humoresque and it was the swing version. Joe Freas Yeoman 2c, took a great dislike to the record. One night, Shreve was on night lookout up in the periscope shears. He remembered Freas asking for permission to come topside from the OOD. Permission was granted and he came topside to smoke a cigarette. He went to the after-cigarette deck and Shreve watched him reach into his shirt and throw a disk into the sea. Ruspino looked high and low for that record and never found it. Shreve never said a word about what happened until he met Ruspino in Portsmouth, New Hampshire on August 17, 1995, for the 50th Anniversary Reunion of the launching of Toro. Shreve said he went up to Ruspino and said "Mr. Ruspino, did you ever find that favorite record of yours that got lost when we were on Toro? Well let me tell you, a certain mercurial Yeoman took a dislike to that record and threw it somewhere in the ocean between Panama and Hawaii." Ruspino responded, "I loved that record. I always wondered what happened to it. I could have killed that guy for that record."

John E. Smith, CEM, Parry, R.T.2c
February 1945

Lehenmann, EM3c, Toups, S1c

Puccetti, S1c, Sparks, F1c
Key West, February 1945

Smith, CEM
Van Auken, EM3c
Cook, FC3c
Konig, F1c
Anderberg, QM1c
Parry, RT2c
Toups, S1c
Key West, February 1945

Cook, Zarnack, Konig

Pearl Harbor

On March 30, while enroute to Pearl Harbor, the master gyrocompass went out. The Arma Mark 7 Gyrocompass measures the movement of a ship around small wheels turning at high speed to track the movement of a ship. During it's time the gyrocompass was the most important high technology equipment aboard a submarine. Without the gyro, navigation below the seas for attack or escape is difficult and fire control systems are cumbersome. The gyro is an integral part of the fire control system that includes the torpedo data computer, dead reckoning analyzer, dead reckoning tracers, dummy log, pit log, sonars, and radars. This was the scenario from the deck log on that day:

0-4: Underway in company with U.S.S. Bumper (SS333) zigzagging on plan #7 U.S.F. 10-A, base course 270 T and pgc. Speed standard 13.5 knots. Battery charge in progress.

0227 follow up system on gyro went out; shifted steering to control room, steering by magnetic compass. Started auxiliary gyrocompass. 0235 changed speed to two-thirds.

0240 changed speed to standard.

0245 changed speed to full.

0247 changed speed to two-thirds.

0248 changed speed to full, changed course to 290 T and pgc.

0249 changed course to 285 T and pgc.

0251 changed course to 280 T and pgc.

0252 changed course to 275 T and pgc.

0308 changed standard speed to 15.5 knots, all ahead standard.

0320 changed course to 260 T and pgc.

0323 changed course to 240 T and pgc.

0327 changed course to 235 T and pgc.

0329 changed course to 230 T and pgc.

0337 changed course to 245 T and pgc.

0339 changed course to 255 T and pgc.

0340 changed course to 270 T and pgc.

0350 changed standard speed to 13.5 knots, all ahead standard.

4-8: Underway as before.

0524 secured battery charge.

0544 commenced by steering with auxiliary gyrocompass. Resumed zig-zag plan.

0602 secured master gyrocompass.

At 1648 the follow up system on the master gyrocompass was back in commission.

As mentioned earlier, Van graduated number one in his gyrocompass class on September 2, 1944, at the Navy Yard in New York. He was qualified in the operation and maintenance of the Arma Mark 7 master gyrocompass, the Arma Mark 9 auxiliary gyrocompass, and the dead reckoning 1 equipment. Spain related to me in March 1998, that Toro was going around in circles because it could not properly navigate the sub. Van and Spain worked on the "repeater" gyrocompass and after many hours with many of the crewmembers watching, finally got it repaired. Van was and Electrician's Mate Third Class at the time and his duty station was in the maneuvering room, and in the control room in charge of the navigational equipment, fire control and the main gyroscope.

On March 31, at 1052, Toro was maneuvering at various courses and speeds to keep clear of tanker. At 1112, an unidentified tanker fired one shot: range 12,280 yards no damage was reported. From 1605 until 1710, Captain Grant inspected Toro in preparation of their arrival at Pearl Harbor. At 2345, Toro picked up land on the SJ radar system bearing 215 T. Range was 55 miles. On April 1, at 0605, Toro exchanged recognition signals with P.C. 484, it's escort, and proceeded in company with it into Pearl. At 0935, Toro set all clocks back ½ hour to (+9 ½) zone time. At 1045, Buoy #1 abeam to port 100 yards, entering Pearl Harbor Channel. Shreve remembers that when they were coming into Pearl, they could still see the devastation left from the Japanese surprise attack of December 7, 1941. To him "it was unreal." Amongst the crew, each man had their own thought and not much was said. At 1124, Toro moored starboard side to Pier S 5, Submarine Base, Pearl Harbor, T.H. At 1412, Toro commenced unloading 19 of her torpedoes. On April 4, at 1300 pursuant to C.S.D. 141 order No. FB 5-141/P16-3/MM, the following men reported aboard for duty: Guttormsen, W.L., EM2c, Oakley O.C. Jr, TM2c, Logsdon, E.E., F1c, (from Indianapolis), Strahan, J.C. Jr., S1c, Stiles, D.F., S1c. At 1500 pursuant to C.S.D. 141 verbal orders, the following men were transferred to Submarine Division 141: Schalbert, E.V., CTM, Speaks, C., CMoMM, Thompson, A.K., QM1c, Curry, D.A., S1c. On April 5, at 1300 pursuant to C.S.D. 141 order No. FB 5-141/P16-3/MM, the following men reported for duty: Helm, F.J. SM3c, Morgan, J.J.F1c, at 1500 pursuant to C.S.D. 141 verbal orders the following men were transferred to Submarine Division 141: Dunneback, J.F. TM3c, Eder, H. G. EM2c, and Konig, C.E. F1c. The officers of Toro stayed at the Royal Hawaiian Hotel which was customary according to Ruspino. During her time in Pearl, Toro continued her training, which included making quick dives, practice approaches, firing water slugs from her torpedo tubes and firing practice torpedoes. On April 9, she conducted lifeguard exercises picking up men from two rubber life rafts. On April 12, she practiced firing all her deck guns in a simulated battle surface attack. On April 13, word was received that President Roosevelt died. It was sobering news for the crew as many of the younger sailors had never known another president in the White House. From April 15-17, Toro was docked in ARD-2 floating dry dock for maintenance and inspection of her underwater body. On April 16, at 1300 the Engineering Officer (William Ruspino) and Ensign (Luna Davis), conducted the final inspection of the work completed. On April 17, at 1000, McNamar, B.D. F1c, and Pendergrass, F.M., S3c reported aboard for duty in accordance with verbal orders from C.S.D. 141. At 1030 transferred Wait, C.W., S1c, to ComSubDiv 141 pursuant to C.S.D. 141 verbal orders.

On April 18, Toro continued her training by conducting battle stations surface firing her 5", 40 mm, 20 mm and .50 cal. deck guns. She practiced making quick dives and conducted battle stations submerged making practice torpedo approaches. She conducted exercise approaches on U.S.S. Florikan and fired practice torpedoes from tubes #1, #2, and #3. Toro had the Mark III Torpedo Data Computer (TDC) aboard. It was located in the conning tower near where Captain Jim would be during battle stations submerged. The TDC was an electromechanical system of two main sections. The position keeper section provided a continuous display of the relative positions of target and submarine. The angle solver section generated the corresponding, continuously updated torpedo gyro angle, and transmitted that data directly to whichever bank of torpedo tubes, forward or aft, was used.

Up to the moment of firing a given torpedo, its gyro angle was kept properly set to hit. The U.S. Navy thus had a system that would point torpedoes at a target as the fire control problem developed. The TDC Mark III was the only torpedo targeting system of the time that both solved for the gyro angle and tracked the target in real time. The comparable systems used by both Germany and Japan could compute and set the gyro angle for a fixed time in the future but did not track the target. Thus, the idea of the position keeper, and its iterative reduction of target position error was unique to the U.S. Navy, and represented a distinct advantage. When asked which equipment was most important to them, most skippers would place the TDC at or near the top of the list. At 2010 Toro commenced taking on lube oil. At 2320, commenced loading two experimental Mark 28 homing torpedoes forward. At 2343 completed loading torpedoes. These were TOP SECRET acoustic torpedoes and the most technically advanced for their time (the Navy used them from 1944 -1952). They were loaded under the darkness of night and under a canvas tarp for total secrecy at Pier Sail 3, U.S. Submarine Base, Pearl Harbor, T.H. Shreve remembers the event when it occurred. At 2350 commenced taking on lube oil, amount received, 3,900 gallons.

On April 19, 1945, Van qualified for Submarine Torpedo Boat Duty aboard Toro in accordance with article 5303 BuPers Manual. Captain J. D. Grant signed off on his qualification papers. Before an officer or enlisted man can be designated as "qualified in submarines" he must pass a rigid written and oral examination on all machinery, piping and equipment throughout the boat. The men had to be able to draw accurate diagrams of the more than 30 principal systems in the submarine's complex entrails. As an electrician's mate, Van had to know how to fire the torpedo tubes, while the torpedoman's mate had to know how to charge the batteries. Only when a man could convince both his section chief and the skipper that he had done his job well was a submariner qualified and entitled to wear the silver dolphin insignia of the service. The qualification patch (a blue or white fabric patch with the Submarine Insignia sewed in with white or blue thread), was worn on the right sleeve of the dress blue or white uniform. Ed Hary explained to me that by rights if you wore the dolphin's insignia, you were supposed to carry a card given to you showing that you were qualified. While talking to my Dad (Van), one day in June 1974, he started telling me a little about his job and what he did while aboard Toro. I remember him telling me in intricate detail the step by step procedure in firing a torpedo or starting an engine. Almost 30 years later (1945-1974), he still could remember the process like he learned it yesterday.

"There are no spare parts in a submarine's crew. Each member is a cog in the wheel, and each cog must do its job to perfection if the organization is to function smoothly, efficiently, and above all, safely." The motor machinist's mates, electrician's mates and torpedoman's mates predominate the crew. These three groups compose half of the enlisted crew. Next come radiomen and operators of the submarine's electronic gear. Three quartermasters or signalmen, two ship's cooks, two steward's mates, one pharmacist's mate, one gunner's mate, one yeoman and several firemen and seamen complete the complement. The senior chief petty officer on board, usually a chief torpedoman's mate, is designated the "Chief of the Boat." He is the exec's alter ego, the link between the enlisted crewmen and the command in administrative matters. He wields much unofficial but effective authority, maintaining order and discipline, supervising operation of the watch, quarter, and station bill, disposing of minor infractions in his own way, and generally ensuring that life in the submarine runs smoothly, quietly, and efficiently (Edwin V. Schabert CTM, at the commissioning, and Allen R. Gresham CTM, for the two War Patrols). Shreve called Gresham a "Slick Arm Chief" because he had no hash marks on his sleeves (each hash mark represented 4 years of service). Ruspino said, "if you had a smooth-running boat like Toro you had a good Chief of the Boat." The senior officer is the submarine's captain (James D. Grant). He is followed in seniority by the executive officer who also serves as navigator (Edward E. Conrad 1st patrol, Robert E. Poage 2nd patrol). Aside from these two (captain and exec), seniority does not matter. The submarine captain assigns officers to the various ship duties in accordance with their experience and capabilities. There are the engineering officer and his assistant (William J. Ruspino and Hugh S. Simcoe), torpedo and gunnery officer and his assistant (John H. Cozzens and John D. McNeal), communications officer and his assistant (William J. Bruckel and John Duff Jr.), and commissary officer and his assistant (John D. McNeal and Luna M. Davis, nickname Stinky), radar and sound officer (John Duff Jr.). In all, there were ten officers aboard Toro and seven chief petty officers. Filling the chief petty officer positions were Vernon H. Williams Chief Signalman CSM (nickname Chief Willy), David W. Snyder Chief Radioman CRM, John E. Smith Jr. Chief Electrician's Mate CEM, Harry E. Michael Chief Motor Machinist Mate CMoMM, Fritz F. Roberts Chief Motor Machinist Mate CMoMM (nickname Snake), Lee M. Neidlinger Chief Pharmacist Mate CPhM (nickname Doc), Nicholas H. Mullane Chief Commissary Steward CCS. According to Logsdon, the chiefs were the brains and could do almost anything that needed to be done or fixed on the boat. As far as experience goes, three of the ten officers had been on previous patrols on different subs while six were preparing for their first patrol. Four chiefs had been on previous patrols also on different subs, while three were new. Six of the officers were USN and four were USNR (all four were on their first sub). Bill Ruspino and Bill Bruckel were both Lieutenant (jg)s and both explained to me that they were "90-day wonder" commissioned officers. Ruspino was a graduate of the University of Minnesota with a degree in Mechanical Engineering and Bruckel was a graduate of the University of Rochester with a Liberal Arts degree. Bruckel said he attended Northwestern University's U.S. Navy Midshipmen's Training School (V-7 USNR classification). It was a four-month duration program at Abbott and nearby Tower Halls in Chicago. Bruckel told me that in the beginning he got over his inexperience by telling his Chief Radioman David Snyder (who had been on seven previous patrols compared to Bruckel's none), "you do your job and you won't get into trouble with me!"

During this period of training in the Pearl Harbor area, Toro fired 22 exercise torpedoes. Ed Hary, Torpedoman's Mate First Class, explained to me in May 2002 the following in detail: "All torpedoes were numbered. Even the smaller parts were numbered. When practice torpedoes were fired and everything was okay, then the Navy accepted that make and model. When we fired practice torpedoes, this meant the war heads were replaced by practice heads made of a copper alloy filled with enough water to duplicate the weight of the Torpex (1 1/2 times as powerful as TNT) and had an air pressure enough to void the head of all the water by a timing mechanism that opened a pressure valve at a given pressure. This gave the torpedo a positive buoyancy. If it was fired at night, there was an electric light as well as a smoke pot to signal where the torpedo was. So, when torpedoes were retrieved, the Navy Department could tell exactly who fired it, when it was fired, and what the results were; either Hot, Straight, and Normal or Erratic. By knowing the number of the fish (torpedoes), its number would indicate where, when, and who made it, and all of its components."

On April 20, at 1822 Toro moored port side to starboard side of U.S.S. Capitaine, outboard of U.S.S. Skate alongside the U.S.S. Bushnell tender, Berth #S-23, Pearl Harbor, T.H. At 2035 commenced fueling ship from U.S.S. Bushnell. On April 21, 0105 completed fueling ship. 66,575 gallons of fuel taken aboard. On April 22, 0935 commenced taking on stores. 1135 commenced fueling ship 270 gallons of fuel oil came aboard, 1,100 gallons of lube oil came aboard. At 1300 commenced taking aboard 7 torpedoes aft; 18 torpedoes forward. At 1445 took on 5 smaller Mk. 27 cuties (homing TOP SECRET torpedoes) aft. At 1715 secured from taking on torpedoes and at 2130 secured taking on stores. On April 23, 1200 loaded 50 rounds of 5" service ammunition, plus various amounts of 40mm, 20mm, .50 cal., and .30 cal. ammunition.

From April 2-April 23, 1945 Toro completed intensive training in the Pearl Harbor area; under Commander Submarine Division 101, Training Officer. The total training since Toro's commissioning included: 226 dives, 168 hours submerged, 107 practice approaches, 45 torpedoes fired and 7 battle surface practices. Bill Bruckel remembers being in the ComSubPac headquarters operation room with Captain Grant in Pearl. The operation room had a map of the Pacific Ocean on the wall that was about 10ft x 50ft in size. On the map were magnetic toy submarines representing the location of all the US submarines and the area they were patrolling in. Bruckel said he remembered that Rear Admiral Charles Lockwood asked Captain Grant, "Jim, where do you want to go on your next patrol?" Being one of the most senior submarine commanders the Navy had he could name where he wanted to go. His response was "I want to go on patrol where it is deep" (for safety's sake as he was thinking of his wife and five daughters) as Bruckel remembers it.

On April 24, at 1300 held quarters for muster, no absentees. At 1315 Toro made all preparations for getting underway. "Station the maneuvering watch." Personnel man the Watch, Quarter, and Station bill. Start and test machinery. Special details such as line handlers, anchor detail, color detail, and leadsman take their stations. "Stand by to answer bells." A preparatory command to the watch, indicating that orders to the engines will follow directly. "Station the regular sea detail." An order given when clear of restricted waters and special details of the maneuvering watch are no longer required. At 1327 U.S.S. Billfish (SS286) got underway and at 1329 U.S.S. Toro (SS422) got underway in accordance with ComSubPac Ad Comd. Dispatch 241841of 24 April 1945, using various courses and speeds to clear channel. Toro and Billfish together took departure for Saipan, Mariana Islands. 1425 set clocks back one-half hour (+10) zone time, in company with Billfish. At 1940 escort U.S.S. PC 569 departed. A surface or air escort was provided for all submarines as they departed for patrol. This would protect the submarine from the occasional misguided attacks by our own forces and any enemy that might be lurking just off our Naval bases.

On April 25, while enroute to Saipan with Billfish, they conducted their daily drills and dives. They were constantly practicing their quick dives day after day trying to completely submerge their boats in less than a minute in preparation for whatever danger lied ahead. Soon they would be in enemy waters as they were now officially on their first war patrol sailing into war. In December 1999, I spoke in person with Edward E. Logsdon F1c in Indianapolis, who was an oiler in Toro's after engine room, 2nd loader on the 40mm gun, and a lookout. "Every dive we conducted was considered a crash dive." Under battle conditions Toro could dive from a running start on the surface to a depth of 65 feet (periscope depth) in less than 45 seconds. Ruspino who was the diving officer on Toro, remembers it took about 30 seconds to get Toro fully submerged. Anderberg reminded Shreve that Toro had a dive to periscope depth of 27 seconds.

The diving procedure from the official Navy Manual is as follows: Two short blasts are sounded on the diving alarm (aa-oo-gah, aa-oo-gah), the second blast is the signal to start the dive. An alternate signal is the word "Dive, Dive," passed orally. When the diving alarm is sounded, the following procedure is followed: Stop all engines, shift to battery power, set enunciators on "All ahead standard," open engine room doors and air locks. Next, close outboard and inboard engine exhaust valves, close hull ventilation supply and exhaust valves, close inboard engine air induction flappers, close conning tower hatch. Next, open bow buoyancy vents and all main ballast tank vents, except the group or tank designated to be kept closed until pressure in the ship indicates that all hull openings are closed. Rig out bow planes and place on FULL DIVE. Use stern planes to control the angle of the ship. The diving officer (Ruspino) checks the hull opening indicator light panel (known as the Christmas Tree with its green and red lights), for condition of hull openings. Air is bled into the ship when green lights show that all hull openings are closed. Watertight integrity is assured when the internal air pressure remains constant. The following operations are performed by the diving officer (Ruspino), who is guided by the existing conditions: At 45 feet, shut the vents and slow to 2/3 speed. At 15 feet short of the desired depth, blow the negative tank, shut its flood valve, and vent the tank. Level off at desired depth, slow to 1/3 speed, cycle the vents (to make sure all air is vented from the ballast tanks), adjust fore-and-aft trim and over-all weight. Diving officer reports to conning officer when trim is satisfactory. "These actions are all occurring almost simultaneously although some individual steps like shutting down engines, shifting to battery, going ahead standard are sequential, the actions are done in almost rocket time," according to Ernest "Zeke" Zellmer who was an officer on the USS Cavalla (SS244) serving on her first five war patrols.

Shreve wrote a poem about Toro, Ruspino, the diving officer, and himself controlling the diving planes while in the South Pacific 1945:

Diving Officer's Lament

I'll bet She's going to be a Beast to handle,
She's going to be a pain right in the neck.
The way She holds Her depth is quite a scandal,
When this is over, I'll probably be a wreck.

The ordered depth was ninety feet this morning,
At least that was the order given to me-
But when we reached the ninety, She kept going,
That She was heavy forward was plain to see.

I pumped, and I blew, and I flooded quite at random,
In vain attempt to get a decent trim-
But the Beast, She was in a wicked tantrum,
And gleefully gave in to every whim.

I clenched my teeth and tried to keep from shouting,
Or kicking a hole right in her vicious hide.
I tried to appear quite righteously insulted,
But wondered if there was some place I could hide.

When suddenly She appeared to be quite docile,
I put Her on Her depth in quite the finest style.
But this latest trick of hers proved to be quite farcical,
She left her depth and damned near sank a mile.

Now you have heard the story of my harried labor,
So, with your sympathies loosened up a notch,
Try to yourself forgive my light behavior-
When someone else came in and took the watch!!

At 0900, April 25, set clocks back one hour to (+11) zone time. At 0941Toro exchanged signals with U.S.S. Grouper (SS214). At 1200 position: 20-45 N. 162-49 W. On April 26, 1200 position: 20-39N. 168-16 W. On April 27, 1200 position: 20-40 N. 174-11 W. 1400 set clocks back one hour to (+12) zone time. During this day Toro and

Billfish made practice approaches with battle stations submerged. April 28 was omitted from calendar. On April 29, at 1200 position: 20-30 N. 179-55 W. At 1220 shifted time to (-12) zone time while crossing the International Date Line. Van's personnel record shows "Crossed the 180th Meridian at Lat. 20-degree N., this date". Signed by J.D. Grant. On April 30, 1200 position: 20-12 N. 174-23 E. On May 1, 1200 position: 20-09 N. 168-37 E. at 0545 set all clocks back one hour to (-11) zone time. On May 2, 1200 position: 19-54 N. 163-28 E. On May 3, 0830 sighted U.S. submarine unidentified bearing 210 T, distance seven miles on opposite parallel course. At 1200 position: 19-12 N. 157-58 E. At 1400 set clocks back one hour to (-10) zone time. At 1708 sighted submarine by periscope on horizon. At 1720 exchanged calls with U.S.S. Sea Cat (SS399) on parallel course enroute to Guam. Sea Cat remained in company for several hours conducting radar tracking exercises, and then drew ahead and parted company. On May 4, 0303 passed U.S.S. Seahorse (SS304) on parallel and opposite course. At 1200 position: 16-59 N. 152-21 E. Battle stations surface exercises took place this day using all deck guns. On May 5, 1200 position: 16-59 N. 147-21 E. At 1928 contacted land on SJ radar at 40 miles bearing 280 T and pgc. (Saipan Island). On May 6, 0530 effected rendezvous with U.S.S. Sennet (SS408), U.S.S. Balao (SS285), and U.S.S. LCI 1087. Proceeded to Saipan. At 1135 moored alongside U.S.S. Orion (AS 18) submarine tender Tanapag, Harbor, Saipan. At 1930 commenced taking on lube oil and fuel. At 2330 completed taking on fuel and lub oil having received 39,140 gallons of diesel oil and 885 gallons of lub oil and exchanged 16 Mark XIV-3A torpedoes for 16 Mark XVIII torpedoes. On May 7, Captain Grant was briefed for patrol by Commander B. Siaglaff, USN who came from Guam for briefing. At 1300, persuant to verbal orders, CSP 162, Lawrence, E.R., MoMM2c was transferred to U.S.S. Orion. Persuant to verbal orders, CSP 162, Russell, V.L., MoMM3c, reported aboard for duty.

C.W.V.A.
TAKEN SOMEWHERES
AT SEA ENROUTE FROM
KOBE FOR SAIPAN

Pacific Fleet Operation Order No. 97-45

On May 8, 0940 Toro got underway for patrol area pursuant to Commander Submarine Force Pacific Fleet Operation Order No. 97-45 of May 6, 1945. At 1010 passed through torpedo nets and made rendezvous with escort L.C.I. 1098. At 1600 SD radar mast was grounded following trim dive. SD radar was out of commission. At 1730 Toro sent encoded message to ComSubPac reporting SD radar out. At 0030 received orders from ComSubPac to return to Saipan to effect radar repairs. On May 9, 0645 effected rendezvous with U.S.S. PC 1591 and proceeded back to Saipan. At 1135 Moored alongside U.S.S. Orion tender at Tanapag Harbor, Saipan. New head installed in SD radar mast by Division 162 Relief Crew. At 1620 commenced fueling Toro. At 1659 completed fueling by taking on 3,920 gallons diesel fuel.

On May 10, 1000 Toro was underway in company with U.S.S. Muskallunge (SS262), for patrol area in the Bungo Suido area of Japan at two-engine speed departing from Saipan. According to Operation Order No. 97-45 Toro was to patrol in what was known as the "Hit Parade" area better known on ComSubPac's master chart as Bungo Suido, Area 7. She was to operate on GCT time (Greenwich Civil Time). Dad's Waltham Navy pocket watch that he bought in New London before leaving had "GCT" (Greenwich Civil Time) on the face of it and it was a 24-hour watch. Toro's orders were to attack enemy forces encountered including merchant shipping. Like all submarines operating in enemy waters, explicit instructions were given in the operational orders to "remain outside of salvageable waters, unless in hot pursuit of the enemy or if required to enter such waters to rescue aviation personnel. Under such conditions, destroy the ECM (Electronic Cipher Machine which was used to encipher and decipher messages), and report such fact to Commander Task Force Seventeen." Uncle "Baldy" told me in March 2003, that he missed seeing my Dad in Saipan and other ports they both were in, always by just a few hours. Their submarines were always on opposite courses going to and from the war zone. At 1503 escort was released. At 1556 Toro submerged on course 218 T and pgc to perform its trim dive. A submarine when on the surface, must be in readiness to dive at any time. This requires the vessel to be maintained constantly in diving trim so that little or no trim adjustment is necessary after submergence. The ship is rigged for dive immediately after getting underway, in strict conformance with the check-off list posted in each compartment. With the added weight of fuel, provisions, ammunition and stores the weight is redistributed with the use of the ballast tanks and controlled using the diving planes. The final trim is defined as the adjustment of ballast while submerged which maintains the submarine at the desired depth, on an even keel, at slow speed, with a minimum use of the diving planes. Following Toro's trim dive, the SD mast showed meggar reading of 2.5 megohms. Several hours later the reading went up to infinity. Conditions of water tightness of SD mast head still unsatisfactory. On May 11, 1200 position: 16-03 N. 141-00 E. On May 12, 1200 position: 19-31 N. 137-28 E. On May 13, still enroute to patrol area in company with U.S.S. Muskallunge. At 1200 position: 24-27 N. 137-20 E. At 1748 mine contact NO 1. Muskallunge sighted mine, reported same to Toro. Opened fire with 20 mm. and 40 mm. weapons. Mine sank after being holed by 20 mm. but failed to explode. Position: 25-31 N. 137-18 E. Several friendly IFF signals received during day at ranges of 40 to 50 miles. These were believed to be our aircraft operating out of IWO JIMA which was 200 miles east of our position.

On May 14, at 0605, bridge lookout sighted mine NO 2 well barnacled. Toro opened fire with 20 mm., 40 mm., and 45 caliber weapons. Mine was exploded by 40 mm. fire. Position: 27-32 N. 137-21 E. At 1000 parted company with Muskallunge and proceeded to vicinity of 31 N. 138 E. in accordance with dispatch received from ComSubPac, there to await further instructions. 1200 position: 28-57 N. 137-21 E. At 1516 commenced circling in an attempt to identify object sighted. 1520 sighted empty aircraft fuel tank. 1523 sighted small yellow life raft. At 1525 secured circling and commenced maneuvering to get into position to destroy raft. 1528 sighted submerged log close aboard. Maneuvered to avoid the log. 1540 resumed zigzagging on base course 015 T and pgc., using arma course clock. At 2035 radar contact

038 T, range 10,000 yards. Manned plotting parties, changed speed to flank, changed course to 255 T and pgc. At 2047 changed speed to standard, 80/90 on two generators. Ship identified as U.S.S. Trepang (SS412). Secured plotting parties. Exchanged radar recognition signals with Trepang who passed on westerly course. At 2345 received ComSubPac dispatch ordering Toro to station 32-30 N. 135-45 E. for lifeguard duty during the night of May 15-16. Set course for station.

In the closing months of the war the major tasks assigned to U.S. submarines was Lifeguarding. The success of this remarkable submarine effort can best be measured by the fact that 504 aviator's lives were saved by U.S. Submarines. The value of the lifeguards to the bomber commands was mostly psychological. Flight crews were heartened by the knowledge that submarines were out there to give them a hand if their motors conked out or the enemy shot them down. Ernie Pyle titled an article about a submarine lifeguard mission that read, "EVEN IF YOU WERE SHOT DOWN IN TOKYO HARBOR THE NAVY WOULD BE IN TO GET YOU." On May 15, in Patrol Area. At 0432 (dawn) submerged (Toro running on battery power). 1200 position: 31-48 N. 136-30 E. At 1920 (Dusk) surfaced (Toro running on diesel engines while recharging batteries. At 2100 received orders from ComSubPac to proceed to Bungo Suido. The Bungo Suido (Strait) separates the main islands of Kyushu (the southernmost) and Shikoku (the easternmost) islands of Japan. On May 16, in Patrol Area. At 0432 submerged. 1200 position: 32-35 N. 135-32 E. At 1944 surfaced. On May 17, in Patrol Area on surface. At 0100 commenced getting Japanese aircraft radar frequencies APR (All Purpose Radar). 0231 contact on SJ radar at 11,000 yards. Range quickly closed to 7,000 yards, assumed to be aircraft. At this time APR showed full saturation for Jap aircraft frequency. 0231 submerged on course 230 T and pgc. 0240 contact on sound on starboard beam went to 365 feet to evade. No more screws on sound. At 1200 position: 31-29 N. 134-16 E. 1948 surfaced.

On May 18, in Patrol Area. 0412 submerged. 1200 position: 31-48 N. 132-59 E. 1954 surfaced. At 2109 ST radar contact on port beam, 4000 yards. Put stern to contact, unable to sight anything from bridge. Night was very bright, visibility was very good with quarter moon and no clouds, and a high degree of phosphorescence was present in the water, sea state one. 2229 manned tracking and fire-control parties. Contact persisted for a couple of minutes and then was lost, thought to be a periscope. We opened contact for ten minutes and then began to get Japanese submarine radar frequency indications on APR. This doubled our belief that an enemy submarine was in the vicinity. Upon swinging ship to ascertain bearing of radar on APR, the bearing determined coincided with the direction of the periscope contact. Closed contact at fifteen knots, at which time APR pip became weaker until it finally faded out. During this period frequent pips began to appear on SJ radar at ranges of 300 to 1,000 yards, probably atmospherics which were certainly not appreciated at this time. 2250 secured plotting and fire-control parties. At 2340 contacted U.S.S. Jack (SS259) on SJ radar, giving her area instructions for patrolling Bungo Suido.

When contact with the enemy is made, the general alarm is sounded and everyone man's his battle station. The captain takes over the periscope and conducts the approach attack. The executive officer is the assistant approach officer. It is his job to check the captain's observations and estimates, and to assist with the mental gymnastics required for a submarine approach. On board the submarine going into action, other officers serve as diving officer, torpedo data computer operator, and plotting officer. One officer is usually assigned to each torpedo room to supervise the readying of the tubes, or to take charge of torpedo reloads. The battle station duties of the crew keep the enlisted men busy. Some serve as members of the approach and fire control party, others as telephone talkers, timekeepers, or recorders. Torpedoman's mates, of course, man their torpedo rooms, and all men not otherwise specifically assigned proceed to these rooms to assist with reloads. When attack and inevitable counterattack are concluded, the word is passed, "Secure from battle stations-first [or second, or third] section on watch." Normal routine is resumed.

On May 19, in Patrol Area. At 0044 SD aircraft contact at 20 miles, closing. Bridge received word that contact was 2 miles, closing. Submerged. 0056 surfaced. 0105 exercised tracking party on 3-ship atmospheric convoy picked up on SJ radar at 20,000 yards. At 9,000 yards the convoy disintegrated into atmospheric precipitation. At 0139 SD aircraft contact at 2 ½ miles. Plane heard by two lookouts and seen by one. Submerged. Logsdon was a night lookout and there were two situations that really scared him. He would see the enemy planes coming but the officer of the deck would not order the dive command until they were about 2 or 3 miles away. The other scary situation occurred at night while you were on the surface charging the batteries, you knew there were mines out there, but you could not see them. At 0202 surfaced. 0400 submerged. 1200 position: 32-28 N. 132-00 E. At 1954 surfaced.

On May 20, in Patrol Area. At 0419 submerged. At 1200 position: 31-30 N. 132-00 E. At 1250 sighted through periscope unidentified aircraft bearing 190 T. at four miles. The crew of the Toro placed unquestioning faith in the judgement, skill and valor in Captain Grant. Most of the time he was the one manning the periscope, giving him alone knowledge of what was happening outside the hull. He would make the decision to attack, to wait, or to run. In no other type of warship, the Captain of a submarine held in his hands the lives of all those aboard.

On May 21, in Patrol Area.

At 409 submerged.

At 1200 position: 32-00 N. 132-00 E.

At 1950 surfaced.

At 2028 received dispatch from ComSubPac headquarters in Guam, ordering Toro to perform lifeguard duty at 32-30 N. 132-30 E. on May 23.

At 2330 exchanged radar recognition signals with U.S.S. Jack. According to Smith CEM, there were usually 6 to 8 subs operating out of Guam in wolf packs off the coast of Honshu (Japan). While on lifeguard duty the subs would surface in broad daylight during the U.S. bombing raids, usually under cover of a B-29 Superdumbo plane. Each sub was assigned an area to perform lifeguard duty during these bombing raids.

On May 22, in Patrol Area.

At 0415 submerged.

At 1200 position: 31-41 N. 131-28 E.

At 1730 land sighted through periscope bearing 280 T and pgc.

> At 1947 surfaced.
> At 2158 SD radar contact on aircraft. Submerged when plane was at 5 miles, closing. The threat of kamikaze planes was always present.
> At 2224 surfaced.
> At 2308 exchanged recognition signals and calls with U.S.S. Jack with SJ radar. In a little more than a month from now both the crew from the Jack and the crew from the Toro would be relaxing together and having fun at the Camp Dealey Submarine Rest and Recuperation Camp in Guam.

On May 23, in Patrol Area for lifeguard duty per ComSubPac orders of May 21. At 0127 SD radar contact on aircraft. Submerged when plane was at 5 miles and closing. No IFF in evidence (IFF is a signal that indicates whether friend or foe). While submerged, manned lifeguard radio frequency and raised SD mast as antenna. Toro's lifeguard duty will assist with the mission of Captain Leon Smith, pilot of the B-29 plane named T.N. Teeny (the name in honor of his beloved niece). (In May 1999, I talked with Donald Cotner who was the flight engineer on the B-29 Superdumbo piloted by Captain Ted Littlewood. He provided me with the following detailed information. His plane also assisted with this mission and provided rescue support along with Toro). Smith is leading the 9th Bomb Group in a 28-plane single-file, sequential-sortie raid down Shimonaseki Strait, the second-most heavily defended area of Japan. Each crew will parachute 14,759 lbs. of anti-ship mines into an individually assigned target location. This is their eleventh mining raid on this strategic waterway, which flows between the islands of Honshu and Kyushu, and connects the Inland Sea with the Sea of Japan. The objective is to saturate the Strait with an assortment of high-explosive naval mines that will float on the surface, or at various depths below. These mines are magnetic and are attracted to steel hulls that explode on contact. The goal is to deny Inland Sea industrial ports access to materials and supplies. Captain Ted Littlewood is the pilot of the 9th Bomb Group's B-29, Superdumbo plane that will serve as the flying lifeguard. They will direct any of the planes that have trouble or get shot down and direct them to ditch their plane in the vicinity of Toro, where they can be rescued from the sea. Littlewood and his crew of ten on board their plane will not be part of the 28-plane bombing raid. They will stay back and fly a twenty-mile diameter circle centered on Toro. They carry no mines or bombs. In each bomb bay an auxiliary 640-gallon tank of fuel is suspended from the bomb rack to give them additional flying miles if needed. Toro and Littlewood' s plane try to communicate encrypted on 4475 kilocycles to no avail. Per briefing instructions, Littlewood's plane has the code name of "Early Reveler" and Toro's code name is "Wharf Rat." In clear channel communication, code names are chosen for difficulty of Jap enunciation, in case an interceptor relays a message. They finally communicate on VHF Channel Queen. It probably sounded like this; "Wharf Rat calling Early Reveler…Wharf Rat calling Early Reveler …Come in, Early Reveler." At 0134 Toro surfaced and standing by on lifeguard station, which was about twenty-nine nautical miles off the coast of Kyushu, covered by Littlewood's B-29 Superdumbo plane flying above. At 0225 Toro is informed that the B-29 named Long-Winded Avenger piloted by Captain Joseph Lewis and his crew of eleven, has been hit. They got a direct hit as their number two engine is shot off, number four engine is dead, and number three engine cuts out. In addition, their flux-gate compass is out, and their gyrocompass is unstable. Toro is informed by Superdumbo that the plane is going to ditch at 32-32 N. 132-31 E. Ruspino said that all rescues were made under Battle Surface conditions if Toro was attacked or had to make a crash dive. Toro changes speed to flank speed 18 knots. The current surface conditions as Grant reported to Littlewood were that the wind is two hundred fifty-three degrees at sixteen knots. The sea swells are twenty-feet high. The ceiling of the clouds is estimated at five hundred feet and the air is damp and cold. The water temperature is 69 degrees. At 0328 Lewis makes his first pass over Toro and the first group is bailing out. The second and final group of men bail out on the second pass. This information came by VHF from damaged plane. At 0344 flare is sighted at 080 degrees T. Toro headed toward it. It was an hour and a half before sunrise, moon was at three-quarter stage behind clouds that covered nine-tenths of the sky. Visibility was fairly good, sea at state four. Toro proceeded to search the vicinity with frequent communications coming from Littlewood's B-29 who was giving the probable position of the survivors. Littlewood did not know the exact position where the crew of Lewis's bailed out. At 0443 land sighted from Toro's deck. At 0509 sunrise. Toro carried out a systematic search of the area while on the surface. At 0647 two survivors are sighted by Littlewood, two miles dead ahead of Toro. Both survivors were swimming in life jackets. At 0700 rescued Sergeant Robert R. Canova U.S.A.A.F., 42105346. At 0712 rescued Private First-Class Charles W. Smith U.S.A.A.F. 36841475. Both men were fairly well done in, having been swimming in a state four sea with injection of 69 degrees Fahrenheit for three and a half hours with only Mae West life jackets for support. They reported that one crewmember of Lewis's plane Sergeant Howard A. Fiedler, U.S.A.A.F., had drowned and that they saw him go down. Littlewood's B-29 Superdumbo had another survivor in sight bearing 140 degrees T. distance 3,000 yards from first two survivors. Toro headed toward him. At 0723 rescued Staff Sergeant Howard E. Stein U.S.A.A.F. 36898537, from rubber raft. Position of rescue: 32-20 N. 132-51 E. Toro continued to search the immediate vicinity for other crewmen but were unsuccessful in their efforts. After thoroughly scouring immediate vicinity, commenced systematic search of area, while Littlewood's B-29 was still in company of Toro. At 0958 Littlewood and crew of the B-29 Superdumbo plane departed the area and returned to base on Tinian Island. At 1201 Toro sent second message to ComSubPac and CTG 17.7 giving results of lifeguard work to date. William J. Bruckel Lt(jg) who was the Communications Officer from Ambler, Pennsylvania at the time, wrote me in December 1999, and said "the state of the sea that day was horrendous with waves 20 feet high, so we felt the other 8 men drowned. We never saw them, and we were lucky to rescue the 3 and get them aboard our submarine." At 1600 contact with a second B-29 which was sent out to assist in search. Toro continued search in broad daylight on the surface with B-29 in company. At 1959 B-29 departed for base. At 2255 SD aircraft contact. Toro made a quick dive and submerged when range was 4 ½ miles and closing. At 2316 surfaced. Japanese aircraft radar frequencies were indicated many times during the day on APR, and one high flying Jap plane was seen according to Grant. Toro was within visual range of Omino Shima throughout the day, and it was certain that the enemy had spotted us said Grant in his War Patrol Report. Despite this, Toro was not forced down until nightfall.

Fifty-four years later, on August 20, 1999, the 9th Bomb Group Association had a reunion in Boston. Featured guests from the Toro were Bill Bruckel Communications Officer in uniform and Bill Ruspino Engineering Officer. Featured guests from the Superdumbo B-29 were Donald Cotner, Flight Engineer and Don Conner, Right Gunner. Special guest from the Long-Winded Avenger B-29 Bob Canova Left Gunner, survivor. It was the first time they all had met since the war. After the reunion Bruckel explained to me: "Canova's wife thanked Ruspino and me for helping to rescue her husband." Bruckel further said to me: "that thank you would also include your dad and the rest of the Toro crew who helped get the job done!"

We Are Weary

313PL 7-30-45 A4583 A/C CAPT. LITTLEWOODS
99TH SQDN 9TH GP.

Standing (L-R)
Claude Caldwell, Don Cotner, Chuck Taylor, Paul Malnove, Ted Littlewood, A.C.

Kneeling (L-R)
Don Connor, Bill Smith, Seymour Schultz, Walt Calhoun, George Warn, Rich Richardson

We have flown 29 missions, the last is with Capt. Littlewood. Our tour of duty is 35. *Will we survive 6 more?*

Air Corps Photo, Via courtesy of Larry Smith, Ed. 9th Bombardment Group (VH) History.

Captain Ted Littlewood's crew flying in the B-29 Superdumbo above Toro directing the rescue.

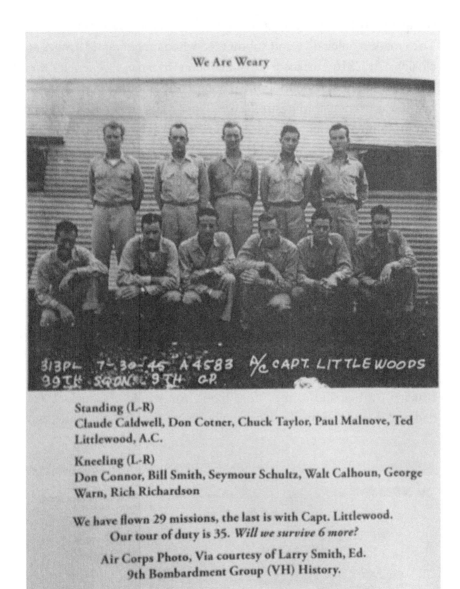

The ill-fated crew of Captain Joe Lewis.

The only survivors of Captain Joe Lewis's plane.
Bob Canova, Chuck Smith, and Howard Stein.
Rescued by Toro.

Life Aboard Toro

According to an article in the Daily Press (Newport News, Virginia) featuring Toro written after the war, life aboard Toro was pretty comfortable. Only the officers would hot-bunk since there were not enough bunks to go around. The enlisted men all had their own bunks. The sacks as they were known, were a mattress with a zippered waterproof and fireproof cover. Toro the dog mascot, showed no preference when it came to bedding down on a sack for the night. He would pick out the handiest one and hop into it. The dog was inclined to give the sack's possessor an "argument" with his deep-chested rumblings when he was disturbed and had to shift his position to accommodate the sailor. He played rough with the men but never bit anyone. Toro knew all of the crew and could instantly pick out a strange sailor who had just been assigned to the ship. After he accepted the newcomer, he knew him from then on. While he was the object of devotion of every man aboard, Toro was impartial in his friendliness. He liked every man, one as well as another. All sailors kept their dress blue and white uniforms neatly folded and stored under their mattresses. This would keep them neat, clean, and wrinkle-free. They had an informal dress code on the sub. The officers and chief petty officers wore khaki or gray shirts and trousers. The enlisted men wore blue denim dungarees. In the tropics, or under prolonged counterattack they wore shorts and sandals. They had air conditioning when they were not at battle stations when they would be rigged for "silent running". Provision was made for showers for both enlisted men and officers. The showers were small measuring about 2 ½ feet by 2 ½ feet and were slightly more than head-high. Logsdon said, "you were lucky if you got a shower once a week". The men's heads (lavatories) are about the same size as the showers except that valves, pipes and cables are kept in there, taking up all other available room. During the day, the sub was lit inside with white lights. At night the sub was lit inside with red lights to protect night vision in case men are called to topside emergency duty or for night lookouts. The games they played while not on duty were acey deucy, backgammon, poker, cribbage, checkers and chess. Simcoe said to me that even the deck of playing cards had red hearts and diamonds outlined in black so they could be seen better under the red lights at night. Grant loved to play chess. Spain explained that there were some pretty good matches between Lt. Bruckel, a graduate of the University of Rochester with a liberal arts degree and Captain Grant, a Naval Academy Graduate and former mathematics professor at the academy. Spain said that Bruckel would quite often beat Grant at chess so Bruckel taught Spain how to play and then Grant would feel better when he would beat Spain. They also watched movies in the forward torpedo room. Logsdon said they could fit 20 guys in there to watch a movie. The one he could remember was Sherlock Holmes. Refrigerators keep stores of food cool and the chill room is used to keep the groceries and meats. Both officers and men have the same kind of food which for breakfast may consist of eggs with steak, ham or bacon, hot cakes, pastry, cinnamon rolls, and the inevitable coffee and sometimes beans. Logsdon said there was always coffee and soup available in the galley the entire day. The crew's mess room was provided with a 5-gallon electrically heated coffee urn with a tap for drawing coffee in the mess room. At noon a meat dish is served as the entrée with fresh vegetables and supper, at 7:30, generally features a steak or chicken. (Once Van got out of the Navy, I don't think he ever ate another chicken the rest of his life). They even had an ice cream maker (Gedunk machine) as mentioned previously. The boat has two cooks and a baker who change shifts at stated intervals because all three couldn't get into the galley (kitchen) to work at the same time. The cooks turn out good meals and pastry. They bake bread when the necessity arises but "store bread" is preferred because it's cheaper and because of the time element. Doing the cooking is Louis Joseph Farr SC2c of Waverly, New York, the head cook; Fred M. Pendergrass SC2c of Gustine, Texas, and the baker is Ralph Clifford Seegraves Bkr 3c of Pontiac, Michigan. Darrell Seegraves e-mailed me a story in March of 2001, about his brother who passed away in 1965. After the war, Ralph Seegraves the baker, went to work for Pontiac Motors in Pontiac, Michigan. The workers used to watch him when the factory whistle blew for quitting time. He used to go into his routine that he learned aboard the sub when he manned his battle station to dive. The boat has three radio antennae; inside phones to keep in constant communication from one part to another; almost two of everything in case one piece of apparatus goes bad. The crew of Toro kept their sub absolutely clean. "A sub is the cleanest boat in the Navy," said the submariners proudly. There's a contrivance aboard that makes it impossible for oil which has seeped out to get to the surface with the betraying oil slick. It is pumped back through a purifier and thence again into oil tanks for use all over again so that nothing is wasted.

There were always funny antics going on aboard Toro to make life interesting. Simcoe said that he remembered when Toro was making a deep dive one day. Toro was diving to 400 feet and then to 450 feet and then to 500 feet and then to 600 feet when all of a sudden he heard banging from the inside of the head (lavatory). It turns out that at that depth, it was just enough pressure in the boat to seal the door shut. Captain Jim was the unfortunate person who got stuck in there until Toro started to surface. Many of the crewmembers had nicknames. Shreve related the best one to me. Donald Ralph Allen was a Seaman First Class, S1c from San Diego, California. Because of his Big Ears he was nicknamed "Bow Planes Allen". As crewmembers would pass him walking through the sub they would say "Rig in your Ears." Another guy by the name of Thomas E. McCay was a Quartermaster Second Class, QM2c from Waterbury, Connecticut. His favorite line that he would sing when he was near the radio room was "clickety clack clickety clack another Twidge in the radio shack". Donald Koll Gunner's Mate Second Class, GM2c from Oshkosh, Wisconsin, had a nickname of "Punchy." He obtained this nickname when he was in a bar once and the colored lights kept changing in a juke box. According to Shreve, this agitated "Punchy" after he had a few belts, so he punched out the machine. "Punchy" reminded Shreve of the actor Tony Curtis who played the light-fingered Supply Officer with Cary Grant in the submarine movie "Operation Petticoat," that came out in 1959. When Toro would hit port, "Punchy" would leave and then come back later with strategic materials that were hard to come by or requisition. When Shreve and "Punchy" were in Quonset Point, Rhode Island in Gunnery School before Toro left for the war zone, "Punchy" left one day and came back later with an electric stove to heat their Quonset hut. All other Quonset huts had coal stoves. Shreve said "Punchy" was "one heck of a Top Flight, efficient guy. He was a very invaluable man and was able to find things when the officers couldn't."

With regard to watch-standing, the submarine crew is divided into three sections. All hands, the captain excepted, stand watches "one in three" with four hours on (duty station) and eight hours off. The work of the captain is going on all the time. He must be constantly on alert and always on call. Each section is organized to man all necessary stations for diving, surfacing, and surfaced or submerged cruising. With the exception of routine cleaning and minor repair jobs, little work is done on a submarine at sea. Ed Hary said the sections that are off watch occupy their time with eating, reading books, watching movies, telling sea stories, studying for qualifications (you had only six months while at sea to qualify or you were transferred), playing games, and sleeping. Ed also said, " the time of your watch was predetermined by the person in charge of your department with the approval of the other rated personnel. For instance, in the Forward Torpedo Room I was in charge, I was a TM1c and there were two other men with rates of TM2c. Only rated men were allowed to stand regular watches except when permitted by the "Gunnery Officer" or other designated official. The time of our watches changed periodically. It would change after a certain length of days, I forgot the schedule, but every department set its own time." Simcoe remembers that there were thirteen Electrician's Mates in all on Toro including Smith the Chief Electricians Mate and that three were on duty at all times. Two would be in the maneuvering room and one in the control room manning the gyroscope and taking readings of the batteries. Max Browning who was an EM3c (same rank as Van), remembers Van at his station in the control room to the right of the gyrocompass.

STANDARD, ON TWO ENGINES

Season's Greetings
USS. TORO
SS 422

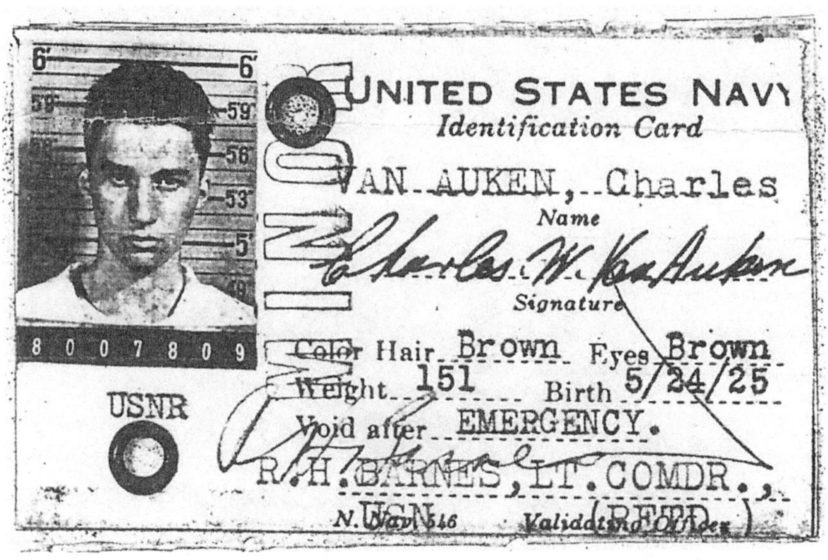
UNITED STATES NAVY
Identification Card
VAN AUKEN, Charles
Name
Signature
Color Hair Brown Eyes Brown
Weight 151 Birth 5/24/25
Void after EMERGENCY.
R.H. BARNES, LT. COMDR.,
USN
8 0 0 7 8 0 9
USNR

Van's 20th Birthday

On May 24, 1945 in Patrol area. Today is Van's 20th birthday.

At 420 submerged.

At 0825 sighted land bearing 280 T and pgc, Shikoku Island. This was day one aboard Toro for her three newest guests (aviators Smith, Stein and Canova). I talked with Chuck Smith in June 2000, and he remembered that they had no clothes when they were rescued by Toro, and that her crew shared with them their navy dungarees. He remembered that the food was great, and they were treated like royalty by the crew. Smith recalled the gilley that Chief Willy would make. It was a drink made by mixing pure medical alcohol which came in five-gallon tin cans (which was supposed to be used for cleaning the gyroscope and other delicate instruments), with grapefruit juice which came in 4oz. cans. Shreve said, "it is a most delicious and refreshing potable." Shreve said that Smitty's nickname was "Appetite" because he was always in the galley eating and remembered him walking around with a can of sardines in his back pocket. Stein sent me a letter in July of 2001. He remembered Captain Grant remarking about all three rescued aviators who were 19 at the time, "no wonder you were having trouble up there, there is nothing but kids up there flying". Stein also remembered the wonderful food he enjoyed on the sub as they were used to having Spam or mutton from Australia. They slept in the Chief's quarters and had to work around the Chief's watches. He remembered Chief Fritz F. Roberts CMoMM, whose nickname was "Snake," helping them with the complicated procedure of flushing the toilet, which was about a 12-step process. They spent their time eating, sleeping, reading and even standing watch topside. Of the three of them, Stein was the one that got claustrophobic being in the sub. To this day he said he still has this problem.

At 1019 sighted two Navy PB2Y planes bearing 290 T and pgc. through the periscope.

At 1030, surfaced and unable to contact Mariners on VHF.

At 1045 SJ radar contact bearing 300 degrees relative, range to target 2,000 yards.

Toro turned and headed toward the target. Smith remembers climbing the conning tower ladder, after permission was granted by the Captain, when the diving alarm sounded. Shortly thereafter a torpedo wake was observed crossing in front of Toro's bow, indicating that an enemy vessel had first located her. "Punchy" Koll wrote me in September 2001 and remembered that Bruckel "pulled the plug" (dove the sub), and they heard a second torpedo go over the bow as they leveled off at 100 feet. He said, "that Toro crew could sure get that boat down real fast when they needed to." Position while attacked: 32-31 N. 133-19 E. I visited Don Shreve in Louisville in February 2003, and he explained to me that the skipper (Grant) was in the conning tower of Toro when she was fired upon by the Japanese sub. Toro was carrying a total of 7 Top Secret torpedoes which included 5 Mk. 27 torpedoes in her after torpedo room, and 2 Mk. 28 torpedoes in her forward torpedo room. These torpedoes were Acoustic Homing Torpedoes better known as "Cuties" that were electrically propelled and were intended to home in on the propeller noise generated by an attacking ship. Grant refused to make a retaliatory move to go after the Jap sub. Some of the crew wanted Lt. Robert B. Pogue (3rd in charge of Toro) to go to the conning tower to take over command. Pogue was well liked by the crew. Ed Hary explained to me in May 2002, that "Pogue was a real man along with being an excellent officer." He was the son of a congressman from Waco, Texas. Pogue refused to go to the conning tower which Shreve said showed his "high character". If Pogue would have gone to the conning tower it would have been considered an act of mutiny. Some of the crew felt that they could have chased the enemy sub and sunk her with one of the "cuties". Yet Grant made the decision in these waning days of the war, not to kill the men in the Japanese sub and possibly put Toro in harm's way as well. Shreve felt that some of the crew was very disrespectful of Captain Jim, especially since he was a proven, well decorated, and an experienced officer. So, Captain Jim took an evasive tactic and dove Toro. Shreve and the other crewmembers agreed that Grant probably made the correct decision. Shreve further said, "Captain Jim (Grant) was a "top-flight" commander and his credentials were at the top and to this day I would go to sea with him again if need be." Bill Bruckel, Communications Officer, also concurred that Captain Grant took the safe approach and that the ten officers that served under him respected his decision.

I spoke with Ernest J. "Zeke" Zellmer in February 2005, who was an officer on the USS Cavalla (SS244) submarine, (known as "Lady Luck" as she was the first "Leap Year" boat ever built). On June 19, 1944, while on her maiden war patrol under Commander Herman J. Kossler, Cavalla sank the Imperial Japanese Navy aircraft carrier Shokaku. Regarding Toro's encounter with the Japanese sub and the use of the cutie torpedo mentioned above, Zeke said in his opinion, "this discussion on the potential use of the cutie against another submerged submarine is a bit optimistic about cutie's capabilities. It had a limited range and speed and its homing system was designed against destroyer type ships making a close in attack on a submarine. It would home in on the propeller noise and depended on the attacking ship coming toward it because its pursuit capability was limited in range and speed. The weakness against another sub would be the much-reduced sound noise of the propellers, to make an attack at any significant range (beyond a couple of thousand yards) would be somewhat dubious. To protect one's own sub against the cutie, it was set to run above a set depth (100 feet or so) and the launching sub would stay well below that depth. Thus, to use the cutie against a submerged sub would only have a marginal chance of success. I note that later on, as mentioned below, the USS Jack was in contact with Toro and with a US sub in the area, Captain Grant would be even more reluctant to fire a cutie at another submarine."

At 1200 position: 32-39 N. 133-19 E.

At 1953 surfaced.

At 2130 exchanged recognition signals and calls with U.S.S. Jack (SS259).

At 2222, SD and SJ radar contact on aircraft at 3 miles. Submerged when range closed to 7,200 yards. No IFF indicated. Toro was between plane and practically a full moon.

2253 surfaced.

At 2302 sighted green flare bearing 040 T headed towards and searched immediate vicinity.

At 2316 Toro sent third message to ComSubPac and CTG 17.7 of the day's activities.

Zeke commented that "the SD radar did give reasonably accurate ranges but did not give bearings. Its 360-degree beam went out from a fixed antenna (a pair of whips on a mast that could be elevated for use when submerged to about 45 feet, but which did not rotate). The SJ radar on the other hand was accurate in range and bearing and had a relatively narrow beam that rotated to give 360-degree coverage though it would pick up aircraft that got within its narrow but relatively low beam."

On May 25, in Patrol Area.

At 0012 received dispatch from ComSubPac informing Toro and Jack that two B-29s will search Bungo Suido area this date for missing crewmen of B-29.

At 0550 contacted B-29, arriving for search of area.

1200 position: 32-14 N. 134-30 E.

At 1205 contacted Navy Mariner plane (Navy flying boat), spoke on VHF.

At 1230 B-29 departed area, discontinuing search.

1515 submerged.

At 1945 surfaced.

On May 26, in Patrol Area. 0428 submerged. 1200 position: 32-01 N. 132-03 E. At 1210 Toro planed up to the surface in order to blow the number 2 sanitary tank. This tank is located in the after starboard end in the after-battery compartment. It receives the drainage from the sanitary drain which collects the discharge from the following: the galley sink, the scullery sink, the scuttlebutt (drinking fountain), the crew's lavatories, the shower, and the washroom decks. The after head in the crew's quarters empties into the number 2 sanitary tank.

At 1214 submerged.

At 1255 sighted crate in water bearing 310 T.

At 1952 surfaced. At 2032 exchanged radar recognition signals and calls with U.S.S. Jack.

On May 27, in Patrol Area. At 0255 SD radar contact on aircraft. Submerged when range closed to 4 miles. Raised SD mast while submerged and received friendly returns on IFF, from several planes in the vicinity.

At 0319 surfaced on course 270 T and pgc. speed standard 14 knots. At 0348 land contact on SJ radar bearing 285 T. and pgc., distance 45 miles.

At 0422 submerged.

At 0817 sighted land through periscope bearing 287 to 299T and pgc. At 1200 position: 31-23 N. 131-50 E.
At 1956 surfaced.
At 2145 SD aircraft contact, range 16 miles. Plane did not close.
At 2309 SD radar contact on aircraft, range 9 miles. Made quick dive from plane contact when range closed to 6 miles. Contact indicated that the plane was keying his radar on us.
At 2339 surfaced.

On May 28, in Patrol Area. At 0205 SD radar contact on aircraft. Made quick dive and submerged when range closed to 6 miles. This contact, as the preceding one, showed on the APR that the Jap had contact with us.
At 0310 surfaced.
At 0405 submerged.
At 1200 position: 31-12 N. 131-56 E. At 1954 surfaced.
At 2332 exchanged radar recognition signals with U.S.S. Jack (SS259).

On May 29, in Patrol Area. Today was Shreve's 19th Birthday (Shreve enlisted on his 17th birthday in 1943 with his mother's permission).
At 0408 submerged.
At 1200 position: 31-26 N. 131-55 E.
At 1951 surfaced.

On May 30, in Patrol Area. At 0142 SD aircraft contact, range 4 miles. Plane was keying his radar on us. Submerged.
At 0223 surfaced.
At 0404 submerged.
At 1100 sighted through periscope, two Navy PBM's bearing 100 T and pgc, approximate course 000 T and pgc.
At 1200 position: 32-18 N. 131-59 E.
At 2000 surfaced.

On May 31, in Patrol Area.
At 0132 land contact on SJ radar bearing 320 T, distance 62 miles.
At 0405 submerged.
At 1055 sighted two Navy PB2Y planes (Coronados) through periscope.

At 1200 position: 31-21 N. 131-43 E.
At 1956 surfaced.

The official U.S. Navy Logbook of the U.S.S. TORO (SS422) identification number, commanded by J.D. Grant, Commander, U.S.N. attached to Three Twenty-Two Division, Thirty-Two Squadron, commencing 1 June 1945, at SEA, and ending 30 June 1945, at Guam, M.I. (Mariana Islands). This is how the monthly cover page of the Toro Deck log read on the first day of each month where much of this information for this story is coming from which was obtained from the National Archives. The second page of the Deck Log would list the officers name and file number, rank, date of reporting on board, primary duties, and the last column would list name, relationship, and address of next of kin. (This would show address at which BuPers may most readily communicate with the next of kin in an emergency). No enlisted men's names were in this log. At the beginning of each War Patrol, a Sailing List was prepared by the Commanding Officer (Grant), that would give name, file number, rank, and name and address of next of kin and indicating what the relationship was (Wife, Mother, or Father).
The sailing list would read:

U.S.S. TORO (SS422) c/o Fleet Post Office
San Francisco, California.
From: The Commanding Officer.........(blank)
To: .....(blank)
Subject: submission of .... (blank)

and read

"The below listed officer's and men were on board this date of sailing": and then listed all the men. Toro's crew represented men from 33 states and less than half were married on this first war patrol.

Dad was listed as:

Van Auken, Charles Willard 800 78 09 EM3c Arthur Hammond Van Auken (Father) 3 Jordan Road, New Hartford, New York.

For national security purposes certain information such as dates were left out. Bill Ruspino gave me a copy of the First War Patrol Sailing List and Dad had a copy of the Second War Patrol Sailing List. See both War Patrol Sailing Lists at the end of this story. For further personal identification, Van and many crewmembers wore I.D. bracelets instead of dog tags. Van wore a sterling USN bracelet that had C.W. Van Auken New Hartford, N.Y., on it and his file number on the back 800 78 09. He also wore his black onyx ring, a gift of his mother, and carried a Waltham 24-hour pocket watch he bought at the Submarine Base in New London before he left.

On June 1, in Patrol Area. 0407 submerged.
At 0947 sighted land through periscope bearing 280 T to 300 T.
At 1200 position: 31-31 N. 131-24 E.
At 1207 mine contact NO. 3 sighted through periscope bearing 197 T, distance 300 yards on port beam.

The rescued aviator Smith recalls he was eating in the galley when Toro went through a minefield. Everyone in the galley just froze when they heard the scrapping of the mine alongside of Toro. His thoughts were that maybe he would be better off being in a plane than in a submarine. Bill "Gus" Guttormsen said he remembered the sound of mine chain scrapping against Toro's hull and hearing a mine bounce along the hull while he was laying in his bunk. At 2000 surfaced.

On June 2, in Patrol Area.
At 0106 land contact on SJ radar bearing 295 T, distance 60 miles.
0420 submerged.
1200 position 32-20 N. 132-24 E.
1953 surfaced.

On June 3, in Patrol Area.
At 0358 submerged.
1200 position: 32-37 N. 132-25 E.
At 1718 sighted three single engine fighter planes through periscope. At 2012 surfaced.
At 2138 exchanged radar recognition signals with U.S.S. Jack.

On June 4, in Patrol Area.

At 0045 exchanged calls on SJ radar with U.S.S. Dragonet (SS293) submarine.
0425 submerged.
1200 position: 32-20 N. 132-40 E.
At 1815 sighted unidentified plane through periscope bearing 290 T. and pgc, distance 10 miles.
2022 surfaced.
At 2054 radar recognition signals with U.S.S. Jack.

On June 5, in Patrol Area.
0404 submerged.
1200 position: 32-15N. 132-00 E.
At 2331 exchanged recognition signals with U.S.S. Jack.

On June 6, in Patrol Area.
0415 submerged.
1200 position: 31-40 N. 132-06 E.
2005 surfaced.

On June 7, in Patrol Area.
0405 submerged.
1200 position: 32-02 N. 131-55 E.
2015 surfaced.
2139 received ComSubPac dispatch ordering Toro to standby for lifeguard duty at 32-30 N. 132-45 E. between 0100 and 0300, June 8. Proceeded to lifeguard station.
At 2145 SD aircraft contact. Submerged when range was 6 miles, closing.
2209 surfaced.
At 2151 exchanged radar recognition signals with U.S.S. Jack.
At 2254 SD aircraft contact, 11 miles. Range opened and contact was lost.
At 2343 SD radar aircraft contact, 8 miles. Range opened and contact was lost.

On June 8, in Patrol Area.
At 0030 SD aircraft contacts at 3, 7, and 10 miles. Submerged. Attempted communication with aircraft but was unsuccessful. Used SD mast as antenna. Aircraft remained in vicinity.

At 0120 succeeded in communicating with B-29 Superdumbo lifeguard plane. Surfaced. SD radar still indicated 3 planes in vicinity. Upon asking B-29 how many planes were with him, he replied that he was alone. We informed him that there were two Japs loitering about. B-29 told us to standby, that he had no news for us yet.
At 0140 SD contacts on three planes, closest one at 3 miles, and closing. Submerged. During this time, we remained submerged. The two planes remained at a range of 6 miles, apparently circling our position. Aircraft frequency was manned during the time we were submerged.
At 0233 surfaced.
At 0300 B-29 cover informed us that he was leaving area, bombing mission completed.
At 0406 submerged.
At 1200 position: 32-25 N. 132-26 E.
At 2015 surfaced.

On June 9, in Patrol Area.
At 0406 submerged.
At 1200 position: 32-27 N. 132-28 E.
At 2016 surfaced.
At 2156 received orders from ComSubPac to perform lifeguard duty at 32-30 N 132-30 E. between 0100 and 0230 June 10, 1945. Proceeded to lifeguard station.
At 2200 SD aircraft contact, 6 miles and opening.
At 2226 sighted four flares bearing 325 T.
At 2358 SJ aircraft contact at 4 miles and opening. SD aircraft contacts also at 9 and 10 miles.

On June 10, in Patrol Area.
At 0008 three aircraft contacts on SD radar, closest plane at 4 miles and closing. Submerged.
At 0043 surfaced. SD now indicated there were four planes in vicinity.
At 0049 SD aircraft at 2 miles. Unable to communicate by voice with friendly plane due in vicinity. Submerged.
At 0105 surfaced. Established communication with covering B-29. We asked him if there were any other friendly planes in the

vicinity, whereupon he replied that there was one besides himself. We informed him that there were also two strangers around.
At 0230 B-29 departed area, mission completed.
At 0407 submerged.
At 0917 sighted land through periscope bearing 000T.
At 1200 position: 32-18N. 133-03 E.
At 2013 surfaced.
At 2203 SD aircraft, 8 miles. Plane opened.
At 2340 received dispatch from ComSubPac ordering Toro to lifeguard duty at 32-30 N. 132-30 E. from 0100 to 0230 on June 12, 1945.

On June 11, in Patrol Area.
At 0402 submerged.
At 1130 mine contact NO4 sighted through periscope at 700 yards on port beam. Position: 31-45 N. 132-31 E.
At 1200 position: 31-45 N. 132-30 E.
At 2007 surfaced.

The typhoon reported forming in the East China Sea on the night of June 11, did not reach the Bungo Suido Area. The seas were rough that day as Shreve remembered. "Before Toro dove for the day she was going beam ends. Toro was really rocking like you wouldn't believe." Shreve was in the control room with the baldheaded Chief Vernon H. Williams CSM, (Chief Willy), who was from San Diego, California. Chief Williams was a "sailor of the old guard." Williams while in the control room, reached over and grabbed the wastebasket "shitcan," and puked in it. He looked at Shreve and Shreve looked at him and didn't say a word. "It was probably the only time Chief Willy ever puked, Shreve said. He only made one run with Toro on this first patrol. When they found out he was over age they retired him.

On June 12, in Patrol Area.
At 0003 aircraft sighted by lookout as it turned on its running lights. SD showed range of 2 miles at this time. Range opened and lights were visible out to a range of 6 miles.
At 0106 contact with B-29 cover that was standing by us for lifeguard duty. On lifeguard station. During succeeding hour and a half as many as four aircraft contacts were indicated on SD radar at a time. Two of these were ours and two were enemy.

At 0230 aircraft cover departed area as mission was completed.
At 0402 submerged.
At 1200 position: 32-30 N. 132-12 E.
At 2001 surfaced.
At 2013 SD aircraft contact, range 12 miles. Plane did not close.
At 2203 received dispatch from ComSubPac ordering Toro to perform lifeguard duty at 32-30 N. 132-30 E. from 0100 to 0230, June 14.
At 2207 received orders from ComSubPac to depart area and proceed to U.S. Submarine Base at Guam after sunset June 14.

On June 13, in Patrol Area.
At 0412 submerged.
At 1200 position: 31-55 N. 132-30 E.
At 2001 surfaced.
At 2331 SD aircraft contact 8 miles. Submerged when range was 5 miles, closing. APR indicated that he was keying his radar on us. Bruckel's fear was always the 100-foot-wide, telltale swath of phosphorescence left in Toro's wake at night. It could easily be seen from the air and would quickly give away Toro's location. In that situation Toro would dive and change course.
At 2355 surfaced.

On June 14, in Patrol Area.
At 0052 on lifeguard station. Voice contact with covering B-29. Jap was in vicinity during time B-29 was on station.
At 0232 B-29 departed area, mission completed.
At 0406 submerged.
At 0916 sighted two Navy PB2Y planes (Coronados) through periscope.

At 1200 position: 32-32 N. 132-21 E. At 2011 surfaced. Departed area and set course for Guam.

422

Enroute to Guam

On June 15, enroute area to Guam.

At 0223 sent Toro fourth message to ComSubPac and CTG 17.7.

At 0722 lookout sighted plane heading towards Toro. Submerged.

At 0755 two aircraft contacts on SD radar. Recognized one plane as B-29 through periscope.

At 0804 surfaced. Three planes were now in evidence on SD scope. Various friendly plane contacts made during next two hours.

At 1200 position: 30-47 N. 136-35 E.

At 1930 exchanged radar recognition signals with U.S.S. Parche (SS384) submarine.

On June 16, enroute area to Guam.

At 0232 exchanged radar recognition signals and calls on SJ radar with U.S.S. Quillback (SS424). Quillback submarine on parallel and opposite course.

At 0915 sighted U.S. destroyer. Spoke over voice radio.

At 1200 position: 27-45 N. 139-45 E. Several friendly planes on SD at long ranges during the afternoon, all showing IFF.

At 1428 sighted two U.S. submarines on parallel and opposite course.

At 1515 mine contact NO 5. Sighted mine at 1000 yards on starboard bow. Sank with 20 mm. gunfire; mine did not explode. Position: 26-46 N. 139-50 E.

At 1632 received dispatch from ComSubPac to rendezvous with U.S.S. Redfin (SS272) submarine to transfer ECM power unit to that ship.

The Electronic Cipher Machine (ECM) Mark II was in the radio room and was known in the Navy as CSP-888/889 or SIGABA by the Army. It was used by Toro to encipher and decipher messages from ordinary, or what cryptologists (people who study secret communications) call plain text, into secret language, which was called cipher text, under the control of a key (encipherment). When sending a message, the text was typed on this machine by an officer and the ECM printed out a cipher text version of the message on a strip of paper. This was then handed to a radio operator that used Morse Code to send the message. The reverse process was used to receive a message. A cryptographic system consists of the combination of cipher machine, operating procedures and management of keys. If the system is well designed and implemented correctly, cipher text can be converted back to plain text (deciphered) by someone with all three elements of the system. The U.S. Fleet Radio Unit Pacific (FRUPAC) was in Hawaii. Messages could be enciphered on an ECM in Hawaii and sent to Toro where it would be deciphered on an ECM aboard Toro. Bruckel said that there was radio silence during the patrol. The coded messages were broken and read by Toro's officers in the wardroom and were only seen by the officers.

The ECM Mark II based cryptographic system is not known to have ever been broken by an enemy and was secure throughout WW II. It was so secure and protected that if Toro would enter water 600 feet deep or less or the 100-fathom curve, they were told to jettison the ECM in waters that it could not be salvaged. They also had to burn the tables and publications that went with it. The system was retired by the U.S. Navy in 1959 because it was too slow to meet the demands of modern naval communications. The ECM Mark II's critical cryptographic innovation (the Stepping Maze) was created by Army cryptologists Frank B. Rowlett and William F. Friedman shortly before June 15, 1935. By 1943, 10,000 machines were in use.

Shortly before leaving on a war patrol, one officer and one enlisted armed man with a machine gun would draw the cipher equipment from its HIGH-SECURITY storage area. There were two lists of cipher equipment and manuals, List A included an ECM Mark II and associated documents (Channel 105), List B did not include the ECM. Most patrols used List A. If the patrol was considered dangerous or in shallow waters, List B was used. In the case of Toro and Redfin, Shreve explained to me that there were not enough machines or parts for all the U.S. submarines. Returning submarines from a war patrol would rendezvous with an outgoing war patrol submarine and would send it over by line transfer (weighted down so it would sink immediately if dropped in the ocean). All ULTRA top-secret messages were sent via the ECM. Today there are only two known ECMs that still exist. One is on loan to the U.S.S. Pampanito Submarine Museum in San Francisco, CA and the other is in Pensacola, FL. It was not until 1995 that they were declassified.

On June 17, enroute area to Guam.

At 0530 contacted Redfin on area radio frequency, arranged rendezvous.

At 1200 position: 21-02 N. 139-46 E.

At 1247 exchanged recognition signals with Redfin.

At 1314 commenced maneuvering at various courses and speeds to effect rendezvous with Redfin, in order to transfer parts of the ECM. Position: 20-02 N. 139-49 E.

At 1324 launched rubber boat.

At 1350 took aboard rubber boat.

At 1359 parted company with U.S.S. Redfin (SS272) and set course for 135 T. and pgc, speed standard on two main generators.

On June 18, enroute area to Guam.

At 0430 advanced clocks one hour to minus ten (-10) time zone.

At 0545 secured battery charge, commenced carrying a zero float on the auxiliary engine.

At 0558 changed base course to 125 T and pgc.

At 0719 commenced maneuvering at various courses and speeds

> investigating an object on the surface. Expended 20 rounds of 20mm ammunition to sink same.
> At 0730 resumed zigzagging on base course 125 T and pgc, speed standard on three main generators.
> At 1200 position: 17-16 N. 143-48 E.
> At 1650 sighted land bearing 086 T, range 40 miles, Anatahau Island.

Like all sailors aboard the sub, Toro, the mascot dog was always ready for shore leave and could smell land long before any of the men could see it. When within sight of land, Toro would start to whine and look out over the sea like a veteran sailor. Toro, an alert and lively little dog, is, in the words of officers and men of the sub, a "true submariner." He was fast on his feet when chow call sounded and would get into his place for maneuvers when needed. He did just about everything that the men do. He was loved by the men from the skipper on down. When he was on shore leave, he was held with a leash, not because he'd run away but because the men felt he could be stolen. Chief Pharmacist's Mate Lee Neidlinger was the authority for the statement that Toro liked his beer, going for the fluid in a big way. "When Toro gets too much beer under his skin, he is inclined to list a little to the starboard, Neidlinger said. Toro can take his beer or leave it alone. Like a true sailor he's always ready for chow call and waits topside to go ashore on liberty when the sub docks."

On June 19, enroute area to Guam.

> At 0522 exchanged calls with escort U.S.S. Dohenty (DE14), and U.S.S. Peto (SS265) sub and set course for 146 T and pgc, in formation to enter Apra Harbor, Guam.
> At 0740 stationed maneuvering watch, using various courses and speeds to enter harbor.
> At 0755 Lt. T.E. Lain, U.S.N. and Lt. J.J. Butlak, U.S.N. came aboard as pilots.
> At 0811 moored starboard side to U.S.S. Cero outboard of U.S.S.

Apollo.

At 1515 eight officers and fifty-seven men left the sub for Camp Dealy Submarine Recuperation Center, Guam, Marianas Islands.

The health of the crew during this first patrol was above average as it was reported in the War Patrol Report that Captain Grant prepared. There were no admissions to the sick list. Doc Neidlinger kept a constant eye on the men's mental health as well as their physical well-being. He was the custodian of the chewing gum. At the beginning of the patrol, each man was given a carton of chewing gum. It is believed that the use of the gum had a marked effect in reducing the number of stomach and intestinal disorders usually noticed during a war patrol according to Captain Jim. Neidlinger also invented a concoction which he found effective for seasickness and had another bottle of something labeled "Dobie's itch," which he admitted was used to treat the seagoing equivalent of athlete's foot. He was the only "medical man" aboard and during his many tours of duty had treated everything but a fracture to contend with among the men and passengers. The food was of very good quality, with a variety of menus and ample quantity for all hands. Preparations and serving were done under sanitary conditions. Captain Jim also said the habitability of the boat was good.

The performance of the officers and the crew was very good. Despite the non-combative nature of the patrol, morale remained high. There were 78 men on board during patrol. There were 49 men qualified at the start of the patrol and 78 men qualified at the end of patrol. There were 28 men unqualified making their first patrol. Miles steamed on patrol and fuel used: base to area: 5,134 miles and 47,930 gallons of fuel used. In patrol area: 4,383 miles and 33,830 gallons of fuel used. Area to base: 1,551 miles and 23,950 gallons of fuel used. Total miles traveled 11,068 and fuel consumed 105,710 gallons. Days enroute to area 16, days in patrol area 31, days enroute to base, 4, and days submerged 29. Factors of endurance remaining: torpedoes all, fuel 41,022 gallons, provisions remaining 18 days, personnel factor 20 days, limiting factor of this patrol: ComSubPac Operational Order to return to Guam.

Grant stated in the War Patrol report the following: Japanese aircraft were the only antisubmarine weapons encountered during this patrol. Their effectiveness attained the nuisance stage, for they forced a good many up and down measures on our part. Toro's policy of submerging when the Jap aviator reached a range of 5 miles, closing, proved to be effective. No aerial bombs were released. Numerous radar aircraft contacts were made while in the patrol area. The efficiency of Japanese airborne radar has greatly increased, so that now the planes will be found out searching on overcast as well as on clear nights. The trick of making contact on the submarine, and then keying the radar and cutting down on the gain, has been learned by the Jap, and it was Toro's experience to observe him doing this several times as he was closing on us at night. Japanese planes were invariably encountered on the nights when we were assigned lifeguard duty. It began to be too much a matter of routine, the Jap being out on these nights, to be coincidental with lifeguarding. The possibility exists that when Yank aircraft are detected over various targets in the southwestern Japanese homeland, the Jap will send out planes over the Bungo Suido Area to counteract lifeguard measures. He may be aware of our lifeguard measures in this area. Two mines were encountered enroute to area, which were sunk by gunfire, and two mines were sighted in the area while submerged. The latter two were not sunk. One mine was sunk enroute to base. The 40 mm. is believed to be the most effective weapon for sinking mines.

The Commander of Submarine Division TWO EIGHTY-ONE indicated that Toro returned to base in very good material condition in an outstanding state of cleanliness. The Commanding Officer (Grant), is commended on the healthy sense of responsibility he has obviously instilled in his ship's company. Ed Hary remembered Captain Jim when he gave the Forward Torpedo Room a low rating

U. S. S. TORO (SS422)

Care of Fleet Post Office,
San Francisco, California

SS422/P16-4/MM

Serial (40)

June 19, 1945

From: The Commanding Officer.
To : STEIN, H.E., 36898537, Staff Sergeant, USAAF.

Subject: O-R-D-E-R-S.

1. Upon receipt of these orders and when directed by proper authority, you will take charge of the below listed men and report to the Commanding Officer, U.S. Naval Station, Guam, for further transfer to the 9th Bomber Group, Tinian:

CANOVA, R.R., 42105346, Sergeant, USAAF.
SMITH, C.W., 36841475, Private First Class, USAAF.

J. D. GRANT.

on an inspection when all he could find was a nickel in the bilges. Ed said, "from then on we were always at the top of his list, best in cleanliness and efficiency."

The Commander of the Submarine Force, Pacific Fleet wrote the following: The first war patrol of Toro, under the command of Commander J.D. Grant, U.S. Navy, was conducted in the Bungo Suido Area. While Toro, on her initial war patrol, was afforded no opportunity to inflict damage upon the enemy despite thorough area coverage, her untiring efforts in connection with lifeguard duties in the face of strong enemy aircraft anti-submarine measures were rewarded with the pleasure of rescuing three friendly aviators. The award of Submarine Combat Insignia for this patrol is authorized. The Commander Submarine Force, Pacific Fleet, congratulates the commanding officer, officers, and crew of the Toro for their successful performance of lifeguard duties, wishes them better hunting next patrol.

On June 20, at 1300 Toro was underway, maneuvering at various courses and speeds to moor alongside U.S.S. Fulton (AS-11) tender to begin her normal refit by Submarine Division 342. When a submarine would return from a war patrol in enemy waters it would be assigned to a squadron commander for refit. The refit workload had to be equalized, so often it would not be her own squadron commander. This was the case with Toro as her regular Submarine Division was 322. The submarine was also assigned to one of the division commanders of that squadron for training. A relief crew would take over the submarine while the regular crew from Toro went ashore to Camp Dealy for some much-deserved R & R. The relief crew would undertake all submarine repairs, short of a complete overhaul, while tied up to Fulton (submarine tender). Everything from replacement of a damaged propeller to the adjustment of a cranky sextant, the supplying of all necessary food, fuel, clothing, spare parts, munitions, medical stores, and the care of all material needs of the submarine.

After a period of R & R, the regular crew would return to Toro. One day would be spent testing machinery and equipment, and in making a trim dive. Four days would be spent for refresher training at sea under the division commander. Two days would be spent loading stores, food, fuel, and torpedoes, and in getting ready for sea. On the 'readiness-for-sea day," the submarine would pass to direct command of the force commander, who would issue the operational order to Captain Grant and Toro would begin her next war patrol. Except for unusual repair work or special training, the normal refit and training period lasted about three weeks. The war patrol would last from 45 to 60 days. The normal patrol cycle lasted 75 days which included the time to get to the assigned patrol area and the time to return to base.

Captain Grant wrote a letter dated June 19, to Staff Sergeant, USAAF, H.E Stein who was one of the rescued aviators that Toro and her crew picked up on May 23, 1945, spelling out his orders. I received a copy of this letter from Donald Cotner in May 1999. Donald Cotner was the flight engineer who was on board the B-29 Superdumbo plane piloted by Captain Ted Littlewood, that ultimately directed the damaged B-29 plane of Captain Joe Lewis's to Toro before the crew bailed out. The letter was on Toro's letterhead (which featured a picture at the top of Toro the mascot on commissioning day), and it read: "Upon receipt of these orders and when directed by proper authority, you will take charge of the below listed men and report to the Commanding Officer, U.S. Naval Station, Guam, for further transfer to the 9th Bomber Group, Tinian: Canova, R.R., Sergeant, USAAF, and Smith, C.W., Private First Class, USAAF", signed J.D. Grant. Shreve told me that when "Appetite" Smith left Toro, he left behind by accident, his dog tags on his bunk. Years later after the war was over, when Shreve was visiting Smith's parents in Wisconsin, he delivered Smith's dog tags to him after thirty years. As a side note, I talked with Chuck Smith in July 2001, and he remembered going back to the island of Tinian where they had originally taken off from on their bombing mission of Japan. He remembered the secrecy and heavily guarded hanger of Paul Tibbets, pilot of the B-29 Enola Gay, that dropped the first atom bomb over Japan on August 6, 1945, which ultimately ended World War II. Though at the time nothing of the secret plan was known.

Ed Logsdon said that when Toro first came into Guam after its first War Patrol, Captain Grant was asked if he had any booze on board that he could donate to the officer's club. Of course, he said no. Afterwards, Logsdon heard the Skipper say, "I'd rather throw it overboard than give it up." Meanwhile at Camp Dealey there was quite a bit to do for the crew to rest and recuperate. There were sports activities, swimming at the beach, parties and booze. Max Browning was the same rank as Van. He was an Electrician's Mate EM3c from Zanesville, Ohio. I spoke with him in March 1999, and he remembers signing up to play tennis with Van. Simcoe remembered having a big party where the crew played softball and ate steak and French fries and even the enlisted men could have beer or whiskey. John Smith said you were required to sign up for various activities such as tennis, golf, volleyball, baseball or softball. He said, "you were not allowed to sit around." Some went fishing, swam at the beach, or went to the bars looking for girls Shreve said. Shreve also said, "the beer they drank had been sent to Guam by unrefrigerated cargo ships. The beer had a small amount of formaldehyde in each can to prevent them from exploding due to the tropical heat. As thirsty as we were, most of us could down only two-maybe three because of this." A tropical drink that was consumed by some of the guys on Guam was called Tuber or Tubah. It was made by taking the milk from a coconut and pouring it into an open pan. Add raisins and a cup of sugar. Leave the pan out in the sun until the raisons are plump or pop open. Strain the mixture through a cloth and twist it to retrieve all the juice. Pour the juice back into the coconut, plug the hole with a piece of cork and waxed paper. Bury it in a hot, sandy area near the surface where the heat will be constant. About two weeks should be enough. As Shreve said, "care should be taken in drinking it, -it is dynamite!" Nearby on the east side of the island of Guam were Japanese soldiers still holding out in the mountains. Bruckel said "the mountains were only about 2-3,000 feet high, but you could see them moving around and that they lived in caves. Occasionally at night they would come down and steal garbage from the garbage cans in the Quonset huts."

From June 20-June 24, Toro remained moored during her refit alongside U.S.S. Fulton (AS11). On June 24, Toro was underway on various courses and speeds enroute to floating drydock ARD 24, Apra Harbor. At 0750 Toro locked in drydock U.S.S. ARD 24 for additional inspection and maintenance of her hull.

On June 25, at 0730 commenced flooding drydock.

At 0829 Toro underway from ARD 24 maneuvering on various courses and speeds enroute to U.S.S. Fulton.

At 0901 moored starboard side of U.S.S. Gar alongside of Fulton where refit work continued until July 5, 1945, when it was completed.

On June 28, at 0800, Julio D. De Los Santos, Stewards Mate Third Class StM3c, reported aboard for duty. Santos was 18 at the time and was from Subic, Zambales, Luzon, Philippine Islands. Julio was "wanted" by the Japs for two years as he hid out in the hills with a guerilla band of his countrymen. He was with "Trigger Squad C," which like its name, was active in triggering the unlucky Jap who could be lured into gun range. He joins Bill Rivera Stewards Mate Second Class StM2c, from Honolulu who has been on Toro since her commissioning and on eight previous war patrols.

Simcoe provided me with a copy of a memo dated June 28, 1945 from the Commander Submarine Force United States Pacific Fleet to the Commanding Officers of the U.S.S. Toro and U.S.S. Jack. The subject was Presentation of Awards and it read: "There will be a presentation of awards at 1530 Saturday, 30 June 1945 at Camp Dealey. Vice

Admiral Lockwood (better known as Uncle Charlie to all submarine men), will present awards. Ensign Hugh S. Simcoe, Jr., USN received Letter of Commendation, William D. Mains MoMM1c, USN, Letter of Commendation, and Bill Rivera, St2c, USNR, Letter of Commendation. Recipients, Ship's company U.S.S. Toro, U.S.S. Jack, and Camp Dealey Band will assemble at 1500 at Camp Dealey. The Commanding Officer, U.S.S. Proteus (submarine tender) is requested to provide a photographer and public address system. The uniform will be: Officers and Chief Petty Officers-Khaki or grays, without ties. Enlisted men-Dungarees and white hats." The memo was signed by R. K. Kaufman, Lt. Comdr., U.S. Navy. Shreve remembered the band was called "The Periscopers" and their theme song was "You Go to My Head." The U.S.S. Toro (SS422) earned a Battle Star on the Asiatic-Pacific Area Service Medal, for participation in the following operation: 1 Star/Okinawa Gunto Operation, Assault and Occupation of Okinawa Gunto—24 March to 30 June 1945. Captain Grant was awarded the Bronze Star in lieu of a Second Letter of Commendation: "for meritorious conduct in action…as Commanding Officer of a United States Submarine during the first War Patrol of Toro. Efficiently carrying out his lifeguard duty, he skillfully rescued three Army airmen. Despite the presence of enemy anti-submarine measures, he brought his ship safely to port…"

On July 5, 1945, Van was awarded the Submarine Combat Insignia with no silver stars by J.D. Grant Commander, U.S. Navy, Commanding. In January 2000, my mother passed on this submarine pin to me. She indicated to me that it was my Dad's most treasured pin from his service in the Navy. The coveted pin was awarded once a submarine completed a successful War Patrol. A successful War Patrol was the sinking of an enemy ship or rendering assistance such as the rescuing of downed aviators. The pin is sterling silver and has three holes in it to hold silver stars (one star for each additional successful war patrol). Van's pin has one silver-star representing his second successful War Patrol. An authorization card was always to be carried by the wearer of the Submarine Combat Insignia as proof of the honor. The pin is worn above the Campaign Ribbons and or medals which are worn above the pocket on the left side of the Coat or Blouse (tops) of the dress uniform.

On July 5, 1945, Toro's refit by Submarine Division THREE FORTY-TWO relief crew and U.S.S. Fulton (AS11) was completed. As preparation for her next War Patrol, Toro took on board 74,059 gallons of fuel oil and 3,160 gallons of lubricating oil. At 2000 transferred the following men to the U.S.S. Fulton by authority of verbal orders of Commander Submarine Division 342: Choate, F.R., MoMM1c, Langley, Allen Guy, MoMM1c, Lumpkins, R.W. MoMM2c, Mullane, N.H., CCS, Stuart, J.A. MoMM2c, Tucker, H.B., EM3c, Williams, George, StM1c, Williams, J.F., GM1c, and Williams, V.H. CSM. The following men reported aboard for duty by authority of verbal orders of Commander Submarine Division 342: Cassidy G.R., S1c, Denker, T., MoMM3c, Keith O.F. Jr., SC3c, Kleinman, D.W. F1c, Stewart, R.E. F1c, Tew F.F. Jr., F1c, and Laughlin, R.L., MoMM2c.

On July 6, at 1415, commenced taking on torpedoes.

At 1720 commenced taking on ammunition.

At 1805 secured taking on five rounds of 5" and 90 rounds of 40mm ammunition.

At 1820 secured taking on torpedoes. Received 5 Mk. 18's, and 4 Mk. 14's.

On July 7-12, commenced training under Commander Submarine Division Three Forty-Two. Held torpedo practices on multiple target group, surface and submerged. Fired (4) exercise torpedoes. Held battle surface rehearsals and firing. Training completed July 12, 1945. Ready for sea July 13, 1945.

On July 13, at 0800 mustered crew at quarters, no unauthorized absentees.

At 1200 moored as before. Loaded 13 Mk 14 3A torpedoes for transportation to Saipan, M.I.

At 1600 started battery charge. Loaded twenty-two rounds of 5" fixed ammunition and various amounts of 40mm, 20mm, 50 cal. and small arms ammunition.

On July 14, 0330 secured battery charge.

At 0615 held quarters for muster, no unauthorized absentees.

At 0635 underway from alongside U.S.S. Fulton (AS11) maneuvering at various courses and speeds conforming to the channel.

At 0718 set course 000T and pgc, speed standard 15 knots. Joined escort PC 596 and proceeding with escort to Saipan, M.I.

At 1630 arrived at Saipan.

At 1632 moored port side to starboard side of U.S.S. Sandlance (SS381) alongside U.S.S. Orion (AS16) submarine tender in Tanapang Harbor, Saipan, M.I.

At 1700 transferred thirteen Mk 14 torpedoes freighted from Guam plus .50 cal machine guns, 40 mm and .50 cal. spare barrels.

At 1715 commenced fueling ship and taking on fresh water.

At 1915 secured fueling ship, fuel taken aboard 13,685 gallons.

At 2015 commenced receiving torpedoes from U.S.S. Orion. Received twenty-one Mk 18 torpedoes.

Lieutenant Robert B. Poage became the Executive Officer (2nd in command), during Toro's Second War Patrol. Poage was from Port Arthur, Texas and a Naval Academy graduate. After his graduation from the Naval Academy, Poage reported to the U.S.S. Chester in Pearl for a short time before attending Sub School. He reported to the U.S.S. Gar in Perth, Australia, and made six patrols on her. Poage was assigned to Toro during its construction stage in the summer of 1944, and was present during her commissioning in Portsmouth, New Hampshire. Ed Hary First Class Torpedoman's Mate, said he remembered Lt. Simcoe and all the crew, including the other officers, liked Poage and had confidence in his judgement and knowledge.

On July 15, at 1330 held quarters for muster, no unauthorized absentees.

At 1400 set all clocks back one-hour (-9) time zone. At 1307 underway from alongside U.S.S. Orion (AS16) on various courses and speeds standing out the channel in compliance with ComSubPac Secret Operation Order No. 156-45. Toro enroute for Second War Patrol. The area assigned that Toro was to conduct its offensive patrol was in the Tokyo Bay, northern Nanpo Shoto Island waters, and along the south coast of Honshu in the Kii Suido, Area 6. Its mission was to attack and destroy enemy forces encountered, to report information concerning movements of important enemy men-of-war, task forces, and convoys, and to provide lifeguard services for Marianas based "Baker" B-29s and fighter planes.

At 1332 passed through protective harbor nets. Toro's orders specified to proceed at two-engine speed to conserve fuel.

At 1337 set base course 288 T and pgc and commenced zigzag in accordance with arma course clock cam no. 22, speed standard on two main generators. Escorted by SC 1046, in company with U.S.S. Sandlance (SS381).

At 1812 released escort ship.

At 1814 made trim dive.

At 1826 surfaced.

At 2151 radar contact at 65,000 yards bearing 075 T, Anatahan Island.

On July 16, at 0934 made morning dive for trim and training.

At 0942 surfaced.

At 1200 position 18-07.5 N. 142-41.2 E.

At 2010 exchanged recognition signals and calls by SJ radar with U.S.S. Sea Owl (SS405).

At 2305 challenged by U.S.S. Sandlance, exchanged recognition signals and calls.

At 2315 aircraft contact on SJ radar range 7,000 yards, closed to 3,100 yards. Identified as friendly.

On July 17, underway on surface on course 315 T and pgc, zigging on arma course clock, speed standard on two main generators, in company with U.S.S. Sandlance (SS381).

At 0135 exchanged call signs with U.S.S. Tirante (SS420). (Tirante was the sister sub of Toro and built at Portsmouth Navy Yard side by side to Toro on building way number two. Tirante was commissioned on November 6, 1944 one month before Toro. She was under the command of George Street and Edward "Ned" Beach Executive Officer and on March 28, Tirante fired a VIT or Very Important Torpedo number 58009 which was donated by the employees of the Westinghouse Corporation torpedo factory at Sharon, Pennsylvania. The torpedo with its special paint job, and message written on it from the employees found its home sinking the Japanese cargo ship Nase Maru. Tirante sank a total of eight enemy vessels during the war).

At 0847 made quick dive for trim and training.

At 0858 surfaced.

At 1200 position 21-47 N. 139-36 E.

At 1600 made training dive.

At 1605 surfaced.

Shreve wrote a poem in the conning tower on the compass repeater during Toro's Second War Patrol called THE DIVE and it went like this:

THE DIVE

Dive!!
The word sprang to the waiting ears
Of four tense men in the shears

They left their perch with faces grim
Pausing at the hatches rim
Plunged into the gloom below
And on the bridge-two men to go.

Clang!!
The hatch swooped down upon its seat
The Quartermaster spun the cleat
The planesmen let their plans run down
The diving officer looked around
And quickly ordered negative blown
"Ahead one third" came over the phone.

Pump!!
A man lines up the manifold
And pumped the water he was told
The bow planesman lit up a smoke
Laughed at some irrelevant joke
While closely watching the large depth dial
A hand on the bow planes all the while

A Trim!!
The diving officer told the man
The stern planes he no longer ran
"Five nine feet" came over the phone
The bow planes took her up alone
A periscope was noisily raised
An officer looked out over the waves

A calm now settled through the boat
Men off watch slept or wrote
Or turned with interest to a book
And eased off to a quite nook
Another dive like the one before

Another day of this Damn war.

On July 18, underway on surface in company with U.S.S. Sandlance (SS381) on course 000T and pgc.

At 0923 made trim dive.

At 0928 surfaced.

At 1200 position 27-00.5 N. 139-30 E.

In May 2002, Ed Hary related a story to me about life in the forward torpedo room. "There were seven torpedomen in the forward room and only three men drank. "Doc" the Pharmacist Mate, would bring around the two double shots of whiskey daily. Since only three drank, the surplus was put in a large aluminum pitcher (we didn't have glass pitchers because of breakage problems) and we added a fruit juice or tea to make cocktails that lasted longer which we shared with others who frequented the forward room. Yes, after each rescue or strenuous task, we were usually given a drink and sent to our bunks. We carried about 20 good cases of good name whiskey in the surplus space we had in the bilges (below deck) in the forward room. I was personally responsible for it, but it was for officers only. However, when the officer in charge of the cache inspected it each week and everything was accounted for, he would give a pint to the men in the forward room. Again, we had cocktails!!! No one was ever to show any effects of the drinks." At 1340 exchanged calls on VHF with friendly plane. At 1809 submerged for training. At 1822 surfaced. At 2100 received ComSubPac dispatch ordering Toro to lifeguard league (position).

On July 19, underway on surface on course 005 T and pgc, speed standard on two main generators, zigzagging by arma course clock in company with U.S.S. Sandlance.

At 0100 changed course to 270 T and pgc. Parted company with U.S.S. Sandlance (SS381).

At 0437 submerged for the day.

At 1200 position: 30-00 N. 138-15 E.

At 1924 surfaced.

At 2040 contacted first of numerous planes on SD radar all showing IFF.

On July 20, underway on surface.

At 0042 established contact with our cover (B-29) for lifeguard duty. At 0410 no business so cover shoved off.

At 0423 submerged for day.

At 1200 position: 30-13 N. 136-54 E.

At 1937 surfaced.

At 2233 unidentified plane on SJ radar at 6 ½ miles. Did not close.

On July 21, at 0425 submerged.

At 1200 position: 30-13 N. 136-54 E.

At 1942 surfaced.

On July 22, at 0429 submerged.

At 1200 position 31-26 N. 136-09 E.

At 1943 surfaced.

On July 23, at 0439 submerged. At 0552 sighted Ashizuri Saki at forty miles through periscope.

At 1200 position 32-23 N. 133-46 E.

At 1954 surfaced.

On July 24, at 0500 on lifeguard station for day. Toro will remain on the surface in broad daylight for the day while on lifeguard duty.

At 0655 received our first call so Toro changed speed to flank and headed toward reported position.

At 1200 position 32-56 N. 134-29 E. At 1235 received second report of original. New cover (Superdumbo B-29 flying above), seems very doubtful of this.

At 1310 sighted numerous logs floating in the water.

At 1330 situation clear, above (Superdumbo) calls for another

station. At 1528 received position of downed plane, so again bend on flank and set out with air cover (Superdumbo).
At 1800 cover (Superdumbo) departs area for base without relief which makes Toro's situation bad as Captain Jim explains (in his War Patrol Report), "since we are out of position due to an anti-shipping sweep tonight (by U.S. Navy Task Force 35.3) due in this exact area tonight.
At 1805 lookout sights object in water and as we pass it close aboard, it is seen to be an inflated blue Mae West life jacket (usually worn by U.S fighter pilots).
At 1808 we are forced to abandon further search in an attempt to clear area of U.S. Task Force due in area tonight.
At 1900 cleared Toro second (encrypted message) to ComSubPac explaining plight.
At 2055 radar contact at 18,000 yards on what we believe to be Halsey's U.S. Task Force. As we attempt to end around, two of the pips (ships on radar), are coming in with zero angle on (our) bow at 22 knots.
At 2130 (we are) maneuvering to clear ships and contact them by SJ radar, continuously challenging (them) by light as they close."
Meanwhile, the U.S. Navy Task force 35.3 was conducting an anti-shipping sweep across the Kii Suido and a shore bombardment of southern Honshu.
At 2123, the U.S.S. Colahan (DD658) destroyer "challenged a "Skunk" (enemy ship Toro) bearing 071 degrees T, 10,870 yards by TBS. (Action Report of U.S.S. Colahan DD 658 Serial 0128 27 July 1945). No answer to the challenge was received and at 2126 I, CDS 53 was directed to send a destroyer to investigate the contact. Colahan being in an advantageous station in the screen was directed to investigate the contact and at 2135 I, increased speed to 28 knots and departed the formation on the northeast. Colahan had three contacts on the SG screen at this time, all of which were evaluated as weather. At 2139 I, CDS 53 informed Colahan of possibility of friendly submarine in the vicinity. Although the

submarine movements given in ComSubPac's report 220923 of July indicated that the friendly subs in the area would be clear by the time TG 35.3 arrived, the possibility of encountering one was kept in mind. A guard was set on VHF channel 140.58 mc. and on 4475 kc. in case such a contact was made. The referenced dispatch stated that submarines would guard these two channels continuously.

At 2143 I, SG contact was made on a surface target bearing 030 degrees T, distance 12,000 yards and course set to intercept.

At 2146 I, CDS 53 requested permission from CTG 35.3 to open on 4475 kc. to call the submarine. At this time Colahan commenced challenging the contact on 140.58 mc. using the call for any or all submarines.

At 2147 I, CTG 35.3 replied negative to CDS 53's request to open up on 4475. CDS 53 then directed Colahan to try the LIFEGUARD CALL to establish communications with the target. This was done and both calls were used alternately on two VHF transmitters in case one should be out of adjustment. No reply was received, and no transmissions were heard on 4475. The contact had been on a course of 50 degrees T at 18 knots from 2147 I, and at 2151 I, changed course to 010 degrees T, speed 15 knots.

At 2153 I, CTG 35.3 transmitted a message to Colahan that contact (Toro) was evaluated as enemy and directed Colahan to close and destroy.

At 2156 I, target changed course to 090 degrees T. Colahan changed course to the right to unmask the battery and at 2156 I, opened fire with a range of 7,600 yards." Toro's War Patrol Report indicated that at 2205 (Toro) still challenging closest ship (actually, two destroyers were bearing down on Toro) with light when at 7,400 yards, his (Colahan's) reply is to open with a salvo that straddles (Toro). Ruspino was the officer of the deck (OOD) up on Toro's bridge at the time, and he indicated to me that Toro fired signal flares and smoke bombs to get Colahan's attention. Captain Jim then asked Ruspino, "are they responding" and Ruspino replied, "no." the Skipper responded back to Ruspino, "TAKE HER DOWN!" (Which meant increase depth as rapidly as possible and exact depth will be specified later). Ship (Colahan) was still firing with Toro diving at 150 feet, using sonar challenge so to 400 feet deep (test depth) and rig for depth charge and rig for silent running. Punchy Koll said that he remembers "Toro diving at full speed and took a dangerous down angle." Ed Hary said that Ruspino the diving officer, couldn't hold that depth. He said that "finally after doing every possible maneuver, when we got to 420 feet, it leveled off and then it was hard to hold her there. The Skipper finally got it to respond, and we stayed at that depth for about an hour until we couldn't detect any more activity on the sonar. The Captain of the lead destroyer was supposed to have reported to COMSUBPAC (Commander Submarines Pacific Fleet), that he had destroyed a Japanese Patrol Boat at a certain time and place and our skipper refuted his claim to fame, because Toro was the patrol boat he thought he sank." Bill Bruckel was the Communications Officer on Toro. He remembered that Captain Grant and Lieutenant Robert Poage who was the XO, were both in the conning tower. Toro's assigned area was a 30 X 30 mile square and at the time was outside it looking for a downed aviator. Bruckel said that Grant had been at the radar station in the conning tower observing the task force and their position on radar. He was asking questions of the radar man and not allowing him to look completely at the 360-degree sweep. What he was late in observing was Colahan who was a scout out in front of the task force and that it was a lot closer than expected. Bruckel's concern was to locate the flares to signal Colahan. Bruckel headed back to the after-torpedo room to help prepare the flares to be fired. When he was going through the control room, he remembered hearing Grant and Bruckel in the conning tower above him in the heat of the moment, arguing about what to do. The decision was to either race on the surface (at a faster speed) to get away from Colahan or dive the boat. Bruckel remembered Ruspino yelling from the bridge down the hatch to Grant and Poage in the conning tower, "what the hell is going on down there" as he was waiting on his orders. Bruckel said that Toro's IFF was working at the time and that the entire incident was whitewashed of the truth.

> At 2240 sound has lost screws (of Colahan). Back on Colahan, contact was lost on the Mk. Radar at 2201 I, at a range of 6,200 yards as the target disappeared in the splashes. Fire was checked and course altered to the left to close the target. Target speed was zero at 2201 I. The SG lost contact at 900 yards at 2209 I. Range was opened and a turn to the left made to attempt to regain contact.
>
> At 2219 I, a single radar echo was received which was approximately 3,000 yards, bearing 015 degrees T, from the last contact. This proved to be sea return.
>
> At 2225 I, Colahan received orders to rejoin and set course to intercept the group. Colahan rejoined TG 35.3 at 2301 I, taking station on starboard beam of U.S.S. Cushing. Total ammunition expenditures by Colahan fired on Toro were 52 rounds of 5"/38 Cal. AAC shells. Toro took no direct hits and was luckily not damaged.

The Commander Cruiser Division Seventeen report of 28 July 1945 Serial 0028 titled: Firing on U.S.S. Toro, commented on the circumstances of the firing by U.S.S. Colahan ship on anti-shipping sweep off Honshu when contact made. It stated the following: "A total of 52 rounds 5"/38 Cal. AAC were expended firing on the target. Lookouts reported possible flashes or fire from the vicinity of the target while it was under fire, but the control officer at the director optics noted no lights. The approach to the target was made at 28 knots. At this speed, sonar gear is inoperative due to the water noises about the sound dome. Heavy spray coming continuously over the bridge and director platform coupled with a rain squall prevented visual identification. At no time during the approach could IFF indications be seen on the target. The following factors influenced the decision to open fire at a range of 7,600 yards. Failure to establish identification by voice radio circuits, using two VHF sets and all possible calls. Lack of IFF indications. Lack of visual identification. (Under the poor conditions prevailing it is doubtful if visual contact could have been made on anything except a 12-inch white searchlight at ranges of over one thousand yards). The target apparently detected Colahan's approach and was undertaking evasive maneuvers."

Largely responsible for the attack was a communications failure-garbled message which led the destroyer-men to believe the target was enemy. Toro was considered at fault for not employing her IFF gear and for failing to submerge as soon as she made contact with the oncoming task force-a discretionary measure that would have prevented trouble.

During the entire war, twenty-eight American submarines were attacked by our own or Allied craft. Seventeen attacks were made by United States Army or Royal Australian Air Force planes, ten by the U.S. Navy and one by a U.S. Marine plane. Nine submarines were so badly damaged that they were compelled to return to port. There is a grave suspicion that the U.S.S. Dorado and the U.S.S. Seawolf were sunk by our own planes while in the so-called "safety zones." From the air or surface, one submarine looks like another. Japanese boats had the Rising Sun painted on the conning tower, while the U.S. submarines bore no identification except the Stars and Stripes, which were seldom flown aft of the periscope rigging while on patrol.

On July 25, at 0059 surfaced. No. 1 main engine would not turn over to start it. The trouble was found to be a seized vertical drive lower thrust bearing. Ship's force attempted to replace the bearing, but this was found to be impossible. Grant said, "this engine was given a 1500-hour overhaul during our last refit period and had since run 58 hours. The cause of the seizure was not determined." Ruspino told me in February 2000, (when I met him and we were touring the U.S.S. Drum submarine in Mobile, Alabama, together) and we were walking through the Forward Engine Room he said, "talking about the Fairbanks-Morse engine, we burned up No. 1 engine that same night when we got shot at (by Colahan) trying to get into position. We put all engines on full throttle, and we burned it up."

At 0500 arrived at lifeguard station for the day. At 1200 position 33- 20 N. 134-45E.

At 1353 received report of downed plane. Set course for 110 T and pgc. standard speed on three main generators.

At 1500 changed course to 150 T and pgc.

At 1510 maneuvering to come alongside life raft.

At 1516 picked up three officers from the British Royal Navy who were off the HMS 86/R5/R86 Implacable aircraft carrier. They were S.Lt. Wisdel, L.A. Wells, and S.Lt. Wise. Rescue was made three miles from Japanese shoreline in broad daylight.

At 1519 sank life raft with machine gun and 20 mm fire and set fire with guns, the belly tank that was floating in the area.

At 1520 set course for 275 T and pgc. Ed Hary said, "I was a Torpedoman and when we had rescue duty we had to have "BATTLE STATIONS" so if the enemy, ship or plane, was after us we would be ready to act accordingly. So, I had to be in the Forward Torpedo Room and couldn't be topside to aid in the rescue of downed airmen or survivors of any nature, so unfortunately I didn't experience what went on during rescue operations." Chief Radioman David Snyder entered the nightly news from ComSubPac (sent out nightly from Guam to all submarines giving the daily news and results), Captain Grant probably would have read it to his officers (decoded):

DIURNAL CHATTER X WHALE AND SCABBARDFISH EACH RETRIEVED ONE AVIATOR WHILE TORO PICKED UP THREE BRITISHERS X BARB CONTINUED COASTAL DEPREDATIONS WITH ROCKET TREATMENT TO FACTORIES AT KASHIHO AND BOMBARDMENT OF CANNERIES AT CHIRI RPT

CHIRI X BELIEVES HIT JACKPOT AT SHIRITORI BECAUSE OVER THIRTY HOURS AFTER ROCKETING LIGHT AND HEAVY EXPLOSIONS ARE CONTINUING WITH MUCH SMOKE X JAP PRISONER REPORTS NIPS BELIEVE PLANE BLEW UP TRAIN X ALSO SANK SEVEN SAMPANS FOR DIVERSION X CERO ARRIVED MIDWAY X

On July 26, at 0045 on lifeguard station underway on course 270 T and pgc, zigging by arma course clock.

At 0205 exchanged calls on SJ with U.S.S. Silversides (SS236). (Now a submarine museum in Muskegon, Michigan).

At 0245 cover (Superdumbo) reports (bombing) strike over and departs.

At 0428 submerged.

At 1005 Officer on Deck (OOD), sights Betty (Japanese Mitsubishi Zero plane) through periscope.

At 1200 position: 33-02 N. 134-56 E.

At 1950 surfaced.

At 2005 exchanged calls with U.S.S. Sterlet (SS392) on SJ radar.

On July 27, underway on surface course 270 T and pgc, zigzagging with arma course clock.

At 0435 submerged.

At 1200 position: 32-40 N. 135-00 E.

At 1948 surfaced.

On July 28, underway on course 090 T and pgc, zigzagging in accordance with arma course clock cam No. 22, speed standard on two main generators, charging batteries on one main generator.

At 0030 on lifeguard station for morning.

At 0240 secured from that station and set out for new station.

At 0620 on station for carrier strike.

At 1004 headed for reported downed pilot but returned to initial point when Sterlet reported she was only hours away from that position.

At 1056 headed north again to investigate flashing light reported in water.

At 1200 position: 33-12 N. 134-48 E.

At 1230 arrived at point.

At 1300 cover (Superdumbo) said search negate so we head back to initial point.

At 1630 mine NO 1 contact at position 32-50 N. 134-28 E. Attempted to sink with 20mm and 40mm (guns) but no luck due to rough sea. At 1656 gave up attempt to sink mine. Fired 180 rounds of 20mm and 32 rounds of 40mm ammunition.

At 1830 secured from lifeguard station for day.

At 1837 sighted part of U.S. Task force so from previous experience, took immediate normal retreat course.

At 2208 exchanged recognition signals on SJ with U.S.S. Scabbardfish (SS397).

On July 29, underway on the surface steering 250 T and pgc, zigzagging on the arma course clock, speed standard on two main generators, carrying a zero float on the auxiliary engine.

At 0435 submerged.

At 1200 position: 32-58 N. 134-58 E. Bruckel said that there was a very strong flowing north current along Japan that flowed at 6 knots and that Toro when heading south at 2 knots while submerged would make little headway because of its slow speed.

At 1948 surfaced.

At 2007 commenced maneuvering on various courses while awaiting lifeguard duty.

On July 30, underway on surface maneuvering at various courses awaiting lifeguard duty; standard speed on two main generators 13.5 knots. Battery charge in progress.

At 0030 on lifeguard station for morning.

At 0340 secured from lifeguarding with no one reported down.
At 0430 submerged on course 000 T and pgc.
At 1014 surfaced on lifeguard station for Mustang sweep.
At 1058 sighted mine NO 2. Position 33-19 N 135-57 E. Mine sighted by lookout appeared to be very old and rusty. Attempted to sink with 20mm and .50 cal. but we were forced to cease fire when cover which was circling asked us to "exercise caution."
At 1115 received notice of pilot having jumped. Changed course to close position.
At 1200 position: 33-20 N. 135-50 E. commenced maneuvering on various courses and speeds to pick up pilot.
At 1203 Mustang circling overhead said he was in trouble and would jump. Watched him jump at about 800 feet altitude dead ahead.

At 1225 picked up 1st Lt. Lee Quarterman Jr., 0-415835, U.S.A.A.F. Ed Hary related the following story about Quarterman: Quarterman was a Texas Aggie. Ed said, "I had attended Texas A & M College also from September 1941 to December 10, 1941, so I was interested in getting to know the Aggie and where he was from. He was a fighter pilot, so I suppose he belonged to a different group than the 9th. I still have part of his parachute shroud and a bullet from his .45. The Executive Officer (we called him the Exec.) Lt. Commander Robert Poage from Waco, Texas, related to me that we were several minutes late picking the Aggie up and that he was shooting off his .45, shooting star shells, had his shark repellent dye out, and his spotter dye scattered out, was checking his position with his compass and sexton, and eating some of the "K" rations. When we approached his raft, Captain Jim was very mad and asked him what he meant by doing all this? Not only was he endangering his own life, but risking the Captain's, the ship, and crew's lives and that he should not only refuse to pick him up but shoot him off the raft." The Aggie answered: "that was the first time I had ever used all that stuff, and I wanted to be damned sure it worked!!" Hary continued, "we had him on board for about two weeks, and he told us we had the best food and living conditions he had since he left the states."

At 1230 Toro commenced maneuvering on various courses and speeds continuing toward position of original report, searching for the other pilot.

At 1412 cover reports we are on spot which he has searched for last two hours. We began our search to the south.

At 1458 cover reports search negate and returns to base.

At 1512 submerged on course 200 T and pgc.

At 1943 surfaced on course 210 T and pgc.

On July 31, underway on surface zigzagging following the arma course clock on base course 270 t and pgc. Standard speed on two main generators 13.5 knots.

At 0140 exchanged recognition signals and calls on SJ with U.S.S. Sterlet (SS392).

At 0442 submerged on course 270 T and pgc.

At 1200 position: 33-08 N. 134-46 E.

At 1945 surfaced.

At 2040 exchanged recognition signals and calls with U.S.S. Sterlet.

On August 1, underway on surface steering on course 090 T and pgc, zigzagging on arma course clock, speed standard on two main generators. Battery charge in progress.

At 0436 submerged on course 270 T and pgc.

At 1200 position: 33-00 N. 134-40 E.

At 1945 surfaced on 270 T and pgc.

At 2012 exchanged recognition signals and calls with U.S.S. Gabilan (SS252).

At 2043 gained SJ radar contact on Gabilan and closed her for transfer of rescued British flyers.

At 2050 commenced maneuvering at various courses and speeds effecting rendezvous with U.S.S. Gabilan.

At 2058 broke out rubber boat and transferees. At 2114 rubber

> boat left ship transferring Sub Lt. P.B.D. Wise, R.N.V.R., Sub Lt. A.R. Wisden, R.V.R., and Wells, R.T., L-A, R.N.V.R., to the U.S.S. Gabilan.

At 2132 the rubber boat returned with two movies which made transfer highly successful. Ed Hary had another story to tell about this particular mission. "Transferring personnel, mail, orders, movie film (sometimes we traded movies with other boats), was usually done at night if we were in enemy territory and a rubber raft was used to exchange people or materials from one boat to the other. One boat would drop the raft off to be paddled, or in some cases, an outboard motor was used to reach the other boat. When the raft was clear of the first boat, that boat would move away from the raft, usually a mile, and the other boat would close in on the raft. This was done for safety reasons, to prevent both vessels from being subject to damage in case there was enemy action. Understand that when you were on that raft, you were expendable!! Except for passengers, there were only two of us on the raft. I was the "propeller" and Lt. Cozzens Jr. was the navigator or skipper, but he never said a word unless requested to." Ed Hary continued, "I remember having to transfer the British airmen to another boat (Gabilan) going to Australia. This was my assignment, why I don't know since I was from a desert-like town in West Texas, Monahans, which consists of sandhills, mesquite trees, and prairie dogs. It seemed as though the Aussies were frightened by the rough sea with waves about six feet high and the fact that they had to board a nine-man rubber raft to be transported to the other boat, especially when it was overcast and as dark as I had ever seen it out there. They waited until they could step off our boat into the raft with the senior officer first, junior officer, and the enlisted man last. I thought our skipper (Captain Jim) was very rude to them because it took about ten minutes to get them into the raft, but he was mild compared to the other skipper who threatened them with their lives if they didn't get off immediately because they were endangering two boats as well as all the men involved. This itself was nerve racking, but to top it all off (as

I explained about the darkness) after we had left our boat, the Lt. Cozzens Jr. asked me if I knew where we were heading and where the other ship was? I said I thought he was in charge and was the navigator since I was the boatswain and propulsion. I told him I was going in the direction that I thought was right and sure enough I heard a loud chomping in the water that was from the other boat's screws coming right at us. They had spotted us, and they were backing down toward us and just a few feet away with the tips of the screws out of the water. The Lt. had just asked me if I knew where we were and when I saw the screws, I told him I knew exactly where we were. You have never seen a raft paddled any faster than that one was. Thank goodness I never had any more such experiences. All the other transfers, personnel, mail, orders, etc.., were just routine. After each exchange of personnel or materials, we were given two double shots of good whiskey and told to relax for a while."

At 2146 commenced maneuvering at various courses and speeds clearing U.S.S. Gabilan.

At 2350 exchanged calls with the U.S.S. Gabilan.

On August 2, underway on the surface steering course 270 T and pgc., zigzagging by arma course clock cam No. 22.

At 0445 dived on course 90 T and pgc.

At 1200 position: 32-47.2 N. 135-20 E.

At 1940 surfaced.

On August 3, underway on the surface, speed standard on two main generators, steering 300 T and pgc.

At 0434 submerged.

At 1200 position: 33-07.5 N. 134-45 E.

At 1947 surfaced.

On August 4, underway on course 270 T and pgc.

At 0437 made quick dive.

At 1200 position: 33-00 N. 134-50 E.

At 1756 sighted an unidentified American submarine, bearing 005 T and pgc, distance 5 miles.
At 1950 surfaced on course 210 T and pgc, speed standard on two main generators.
At 1955 commenced battery charge.

On August 5, underway on course 270 T and pgc.
At 0441 made quick dive on course 270 T and pgc.
At 1200 position: 32-42 N 135-08 E.
At 1947 surfaced.
At 2005 first of numerous unidentified SJ contacts.
At 2300 on lifeguard station for bomber raid.

On August 6, 1945, underway on course 270 T and pgc, zigzagging by the arma course clock cam No. 22. Speed standard on two main generators, battery charge in progress. At 0000 changed base course to 180 T and pgc. As "Uncle Charlie" (Rear Admiral Charles A. Lockwood the foremost commander of the U.S. submarine forces in the Pacific at the time), wrote in his book Sink 'Em All in 1951, "Events were marching swiftly forward and on August 7, Task Force 38 was scheduled to strike Kyushu. Our lifeguards (submarines) were to take their stations close inshore after dark on the day before (August 6). About 6 P.M. August 6, a message was teletyped to my office saying the strike was cancelled. This was nothing unusual, but the concluding part of the message directed withdrawal of all ships to positions not less than 100 miles from the coasts of Kyushu (Japan). That puzzled us and after dinner I told Commander "Bub" Ward, the staff Duty Officer, to hop in a boat and see if he could find out at Cincpac's office the reason for that last provision and how long it would remain in force. Plans for the big invasion, Operation Olympic, had already been issued to Force Commanders and one of our jobs was to spot all minefields so the sweepers could go to work without delay. "Bub" returned after a lengthy stay and reported that he could find out nothing-nobody knew anything more than just what the message said.

He evidently felt they were holding out on him for he added, "I think it will take at least a Vice Admiral to find out anything about it." I made a note in my little black book to take the matter up with the Big Boss the next morning but that was never necessary." Precisely 17 minutes after midnight on 06 August 1945, the B-29 Enola Gay piloted by Colonel Paul Tibbets released a bomb over Japan. It detonated 43 seconds later. On 9 August, the B-29, Bock's Car, unleashed a second atomic bomb. These two nuclear devices are credited with ending the war in the Pacific Theater, thereby saving the lives of many thousands of American and Allied troops who would have been called upon to invade the Japanese mainland. Lockwood further said, "undoubtedly a few people at Cincpac HQ knew about the A-bomb. But to the lower echelons, including myself, it was a complete surprise." On August 18, 2001, my brother-law Mark C. Smith (a pilot himself), and I had the honor of meeting General Paul Tibbets, pilot of the Enola Gay at the reunion of the U.S.S. Indianapolis in Indianapolis, Indiana. (Mark and I serve on the U.S.S. Indianapolis Museum Task Force Committee). The U.S.S. Indianapolis (CA-35) carried the components of the first atomic bomb (that Tibbets dropped), from San Francisco and delivered it on July 26 to Tinian Island where the Enola Gay plane was based. On July 30, 1945 at about 14 minutes after midnight, halfway between Guam and Leyte, the Japanese submarine I-58 fired six torpedoes and two struck and sank the heavy cruiser Indianapolis after 12 minutes. Only 317 men survived out of 1197 aboard. (General Paul Tibbets signed his name to my copy of Toro's Deck Log of August 6, 1945). Meanwhile back on Toro, no men of her crew knew what had happened that day and no one felt any sensation from the bomb Tibbets dropped on Hiroshima that day. At 0420 secured from lifeguarding and changed base course to 170 T and pgc. At 0440 dived on course 180 T and pgc. At 1200 position: 32-52 N. 134-53 E. At 1950 surfaced on course 180 T and pgc. Ironically on this day the last U.S. submarine in WWII was sunk. The U.S.S. Bullhead (SS332) was sunk by a Japanese plane that dropped a depth charge on her with all 84 sailors meeting their death.

On August 7, underway on surface, steering 270 T and pgc., speed standard on two main generators, zigzagging.

At 0432 dove on course 270 T and pgc.

At 0520 sighted land through periscope bearing 310 T, Shikoku Island.

At 0600 sighted land through periscope bearing 025 T, Honshu Island.

At 1200 position: 33-00 N. 134-50 E.

At 1947 surfaced on course 270 T and pgc.

On August 8, underway on surface zigzagging by arma course clock on base course 090 T and pgc.

At 0030 on lifeguard station. Numerous planes on SD radar.

At 0420 secured from lifeguard without one contacting cover. Believe he didn't show up tonight as we were able to communicate with other planes.

At 0525 submerged to await next duty starting at 0900.

At 0916 surfaced on course 270 T and pgc, speed standard on three main generators.

At 0933 sighted dense black smoke on horizon and received call from our cover informing us that a plane had gone down and the pilot was in his life raft.

At 0938 changed speed to full on two main generators.

At 0945 commenced maneuvering on various courses and speeds to pick up a fighter pilot.

At 0950 picked up 1st Lt. Paul E. Schurr, U.S.A., 0-767402, U.S.A.A.F. from midst of impressive array of smoke display. Received notice of second pilot standing by to bail out when we were ready.

At 0955 commenced maneuvering on various courses and speeds to pick up fighter pilot.

At 1003 watched second pilot jump.

At 1010 picked up Major Paul R. Wignell, U.S.A.A.F., 0-409786.

At 1030 secured with today's catch when cover informs us that strike is over and no one else down.

At 1045 submerged on course 180 T and pgc.

At 1200 position 33-13 N. 135-56 E.

At 2000 surfaced on course 210 T and pgc. Ed Hary recalled, "as for the two downed airmen, there was an officer and a Sgt. who I think had hit the silk with another airman that had been a true friend and companion of his from the time they were in kindergarten, grammar, grade, high school, two years in college, and two years in the Air Force. Some (of Toro's crew) thought he was scared and wouldn't talk to anyone. After a few days, I got him to tell the story that his buddy didn't believe that we had a submarine every sixty miles around the coast of Japan for rescue as well as destruction of the enemy. He said that his buddy couldn't swim and that he had told him to get in the one-man raft they shared. After a few minutes his buddy told him he was feeling all right and for them to change places for a while. We were some time getting to them as we had been looking for another flier who was some distance from the others. After several minutes, maybe twenty, we went to where the two had gone down and there was only one left. He said he had gotten in the raft and had not taken his Mae West lifejacket off when his buddy said, "I'll see you" and turned loose and down he went. He said, "I couldn't go deep because of my life preserver and had to give up. I never saw him again." This is why he was reluctant to talk." Ed said, "he couldn't tell his story without tearful emotion and I felt the same way myself."

On August 9, underway on surface steering 270 T and pgc. Zigzagging on arma course clock. Speed standard on two main generators.

At 0435 submerged on course 270 T and pgc.

At 0445 Martino, Angelo A. MoMM3c, 820 91 78, USNR., cut back of right hand about 1/8" deep and 1" long while operating ventilation flapper in Engine Room which broke. Treated by PhM. (Doc), cut closed with two clamps.

At 1200 position: 32-45 N. 134-38 E.
At 1905 sighted land through periscope bearing 312 T and pgc.
At 1948 surfaced.

On August 10, underway on base course 270 T and pgc.
At 0441 submerged. At 0702 mine contact NO. 3. Position 32-56 N. 134-52 E. Sighted bright and shining mine through scope. At 1200 position: 32-55 N. 134-56 E.
At 1947 surfaced.
At 2116 exchanged recognition signal and calls with U.S.S. Tigrone (SS419).

On August 11, underway on surface steering 180 T and pgc.
At 0030 on lifeguard station for (B-29) mining mission.
At 0400 secured from lifeguard station as cover reports all clear.
At 0445 submerged.
At 1200 position: 32-56 N. 134-59 E.
At 1947 surfaced.

On August 12, underway on surface steering course 090 T and pgc.
At 0436 submerged.
At 1200 position: 33-04 N. 134-56 E.
At 1944 surfaced.

On August 13, underway on surface.
At 0438 submerged.
At 1330 mine contact NO. 4. Position 33-04.5 N. 134 –50 E. Sighted by O.O.D. (officer of the deck), through periscope. Seemed to be in good shape.
At 1943 surfaced.

On August 14, underway on base course 090 T and pgc.
At 0453 submerged.
At 0800 mine contact NO. 5. Position: 33-10.2 N. 134-50 E.

Sighted through periscope by O.O. D.
At 1200 position: 33-15 N. 134-53 E.
At 1943 surfaced.
At 2352 commenced maneuvering on various courses on lifeguard station.

On August 15, 1945, at 0000 on station for lifeguard duty during (B-29) mining mission.
At 0340 secured from lifeguard station as cover reports all clear and departs for base.
At 0434 submerged.
At 1200 position: 33-08 N. 135-12 E.
At 1924 surfaced.

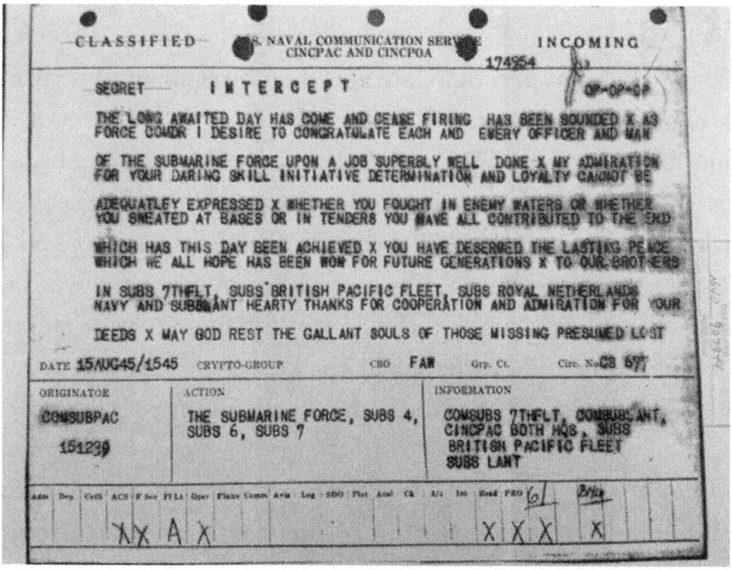

CLASSIFIED — U.S. NAVAL COMMUNICATION SERVICE — CINCPAC AND CINCPOA — INCOMING
174954
SECRET — INTERCEPT — OP-OP-OP

THE LONG AWAITED DAY HAS COME AND CEASE FIRING HAS BEEN SOUNDED X AS FORCE COMDR I DESIRE TO CONGRATULATE EACH AND EVERY OFFICER AND MAN OF THE SUBMARINE FORCE UPON A JOB SUPERBLY WELL DONE X MY ADMIRATION FOR YOUR DARING SKILL INITIATIVE DETERMINATION AND LOYALTY CANNOT BE ADEQUATLEY EXPRESSED X WHETHER YOU FOUGHT IN ENEMY WATERS OR WHETHER YOU SWEATED AT BASES OR IN TENDERS YOU HAVE ALL CONTRIBUTED TO THE END WHICH HAS THIS DAY BEEN ACHIEVED X YOU HAVE DESERVED THE LASTING PEACE WHICH WE ALL HOPE HAS BEEN WON FOR FUTURE GENERATIONS X TO OUR BROTHERS IN SUBS 7THFLT, SUBS BRITISH PACIFIC FLEET, SUBS ROYAL NETHERLANDS NAVY AND SUBSLANT HEARTY THANKS FOR COOPERATION AND ADMIRATION FOR YOUR DEEDS X MAY GOD REST THE GALLANT SOULS OF THOSE MISSING PRESUMED LOST

DATE 15AUG45/1545 CRYPTO-GROUP CBO FAW Grp. Ct. Circ. No. CS 67

ORIGINATOR	ACTION	INFORMATION
COMSUBPAC 151239	THE SUBMARINE FORCE, SUBS 4, SUBS 6, SUBS 7	COMSUBS 7THFLT, COMSUBSLANT, CINCPAC BOTH HQS, SUBS BRITISH PACIFIC FLEET SUBS LANT

Message sent to all submarines on War Patrol from ComSubPac announcing the war is over.

On Van's Navy Personnel Records, it read "in accordance with ALPAC-145-45 total points computed as of 15 August 1945, 21 ½ pts. And witnessed by R.B. Poage, Lieutenant, USN Executive Officer. On August 12, 1995, Mark Smith and I went with our Father-in-law Stanley Stanich (WWII Navy Vet), to a 50th Anniversary Party of V-J Day Minus Three Days celebrated in Hangar 592 at Grissom Air Refueling Base in Indiana, sponsored by the Grissom Memorial Chapter #152 of the Air Force Association.

On August 16, underway on surface on base course 270 T and pgc., standard speed on two main generators, 12 knots. The O.O.D. for the 0-4: watch was Lieut (jg), W.J. Bruckel USNR, Communications Officer, and he was the one who received the ComSubPac dispatch at 0130 ordering Toro to depart for Guam. (The War was finally over as Japan agreed to surrender). Simcoe told me that Bruckel, then went and woke up Captain Jim to explain the new orders. Toro changed course to 150 T and pgc. Standard speed on three main generators. At 0158 changed course to 125 T and pgc. With the cease fire announcement on the (1MC) general announcing system, Shreve said the crew "spliced the main brace," which meant "the War is over, and everything is secure, drink!" The crew broke out the booze and had a drink. Shreve said he was in the Control Room when the word came. He said, "there was stunned silence, and looking at your shipmates, they looked different. Nothing had changed, you were still at sea and you were still in danger. Yet the reality of the moment was hard to set in".

At 1058 sighted mine contact NO. 6, bearing 180 T and pgc. position: 31-25 N. 136-56 E. Commenced maneuvering to explode. At 1103 mine exploded by 40mm.

At 1145 sighted mine contact NO. 7, bearing 140 T and pgc. position: 31-19 N. 137-04 E.

At 1153 mine exploded by 20mm, resumed zigzagging on base course 130 T and pgc.

At 1257 mine contact NO. 8 sighted position: 31-08 N. 137-19 E.

At 1302 exploded by 20mm hit.
At 1552 sighted mine contact NO. 9, maneuvered at various courses and speeds to fire on mine, position: 30-48 N. 137-59 E.
At 1559 sank mine by 20mm and 40mm gunfire. Shreve said that Captain Grant liked to use the 50 caliber Thompson machine gun on the mines and was very good at putting holes in them. Toro was underway as before and at 1600 set base course 130 T and pgc, zigzagging.
At 2215 exchanged recognition signals with U.S.S. Devilfish (SS292) bearing 120 T and pgc.

On August 17, enroute to Guam. At 1200 position: 26-24 N. 139-32 E. Simcoe said that Captain Jim had him write up a great number of maintenance work orders for Toro to be completed by the refit crew in Midway. The reason was that Captain Jim had now just completed 10 war patrols on 6 different submarines and wanted to go home. He did not want to be delayed by having to take Toro to the formal surrender of the Japanese Imperial Government that was scheduled for September 2, 1945, aboard the U.S.S. Missouri (BB-63) in Tokyo Bay.

On August 18, enroute to Guam. At 1200 position 20-23 N. 140-08 E. Ed Hary recalled another story after the war was declared over. "My Gunnery Officer was Lt. McNeal who I liked pretty well. One day he came to me with two legal-sized sheets of paper with all the routine maintenance requests of the torpedoes we were supposed to perform until we returned to base. I took the papers, wadded them up, threw them in the trash can (that wasn't what we called it), and didn't say one word to him. I could see he was mad and was going to the wardroom to write up specifications to put me on report. I got on the intercom and called "Bridge... Forward Torpedo Room... Bridge Aye!! (Pogue)... Permission to routine fish (short for torpedoes) forward?..."Why do you want permission to routine fish?...I have orders to routine them...Who gave you those orders?...My Gunnery

Officer!…Send that so and so to me!!!…I went to the ward room and told Mr. McNeal that the Exec (Pogue) wanted him on the bridge. I got under the ladder to the conning tower which was just below the bridge and listened to the Exec tell him that the war was over, and he was certain that when we got back to port, all the ammunition would be turned in and probably would be destroyed. He also told him the forward torpedo room had been first in every Captain's inspection except one, in which all he found was a nickel in the bilges. He said for him to leave us alone and let us enjoy what little time we had left (together). The Lt. never spoke to me again, and that was the only disagreement I ever had with an officer."

On August 19, enroute to Guam. Underway on course 132 T and pgc, zigzagging on arma course clock, (still taking all precautions while in enemy waters in case the enemy did not get the message that the hostilities were all but over), standard speed on one main generator, 11 knots. Bruckel said that on their way back to Guam Toro made sound contact with another unidentified sub. They tracked the sub for 7 to 8 hours. It finally went away but they never found out if it was an American or Japanese sub. At 1200 position: 17-22 N. 144-18 E. At 2235 exchanged calls with U.S.S. Gar (SS206) and U.S.S. Sennett (SS408).

On August 20, enroute to Guam, underway on base course 197 T and pgc., standard speed on two main generators. While Toro was on its long homeward bound trip, Bruckel said that he got Freas Yeoman Second Class Y2c, to send out law school admission applications for him. By the time Bruckel got back home he was accepted to Harvard Law School (which he later attended and graduated from).

At 0258 (K) exchanged calls with U.S.S. Peto (SS265). At 0450 (K) exchanged calls with U.S.S. Perch (SS313).

At 0547 exchanged calls with assigned escort SC 1325 proceeding to Apra Harbor, Guam. Maneuvering at various courses and speeds maintaining station astern of escort. (I have a video of Toro that was made from a movie that Simcoe shot at the time showing the rescues Toro made as well as the destruction of mines during her Second War Patrol. It shows Toro, the mascot dog, and some of her smiling crew including Simcoe smoking a cigar, and some of the rescued aviators as she is coming into Guam. He obtained it when Toro was mothballed and stationed in reserve after the war in New London). At 0800 inspected magazine and smokeless powder samples (which was a daily routine), conditions normal. Commander K.R. Wheland, U.S.N., came aboard as pilot. Lt. W.J. Rogers, U.S.N., came aboard.

At 0907 maneuvered on various courses and speeds standing in Apra Harbor Channel. At 0921 moored starboard side to U.S.S. Manta, alongside U.S.S. Blackfish, U.S.S. Dentuda and U.S.S. Fulton (submarine tender) in Apra Harbor, Guam, M.I. Ships present; various units of Allied Fleet.

At 0940 U.S.S. Perch moored starboard side to our port side.

At 1150 commenced fueling ship from U.S.S. Fulton. Took on board 1715 gallons lube oil and 79,059 gallons of fuel oil.

Captain Grant wrote the following in his Second War Patrol Report:

The health of the crew during the patrol was average.

The food aboard was ample with a variety of menus.

The number of men detached after previous patrol 11.

The number of men on board during patrol 76.

The number of men qualified at start of patrol 64.

The number of men qualified at the end of patrol 67.

The number of unqualified men making their first patrol 9.

Miles steamed: Guam to area 1,320 miles, 16,250 gallons of fuel used. In area 5,610 miles, 48,290 gallons of fuel used. Area to Guam 1,200 miles, 24,280 gallons of fuel used.

Duration of patrol:

Days enroute to area 3.

Days in area 28. Days enroute to base 4.

Days submerged 25.

Factors of endurance remaining:
Torpedoes 29,
Fuel 25,000 gallons,
Provisions 30 days,
personnel factor 30 days, limiting factor this patrol,
ComSubPac dispatch orders (War ended).

On August 28, the Commander Submarine Division Three Twenty-Two stated in his report that Toro was very clean and in good material condition on arrival in Midway. It is expected that a modified refit can be accomplished in a seven-day period and she will be ready for sea redeployment. The Division congratulates the Commanding Officer (Grant), officers and crew on the completion of this patrol, and on the rescue of six aviators.

On September 24, 1945, the Commander Submarine Force, Pacific Fleet concluded the following: The Second War Patrol of the U.S.S. Toro, under the command of Commander J.D. Grant, U.S. Navy, was conducted in the approaches to the Kii Suido. No enemy shipping was sighted hence no attacks were made. Toro proved to be an alert lifeguard, rescuing three officers of the Royal Navy and three of the U.S.A.A.F. in four well conducted recoveries. The unfortunate embroilment with our own anti-shipping sweep on the night of 24 July resulted in no material damage. The Toro was unopposed by the enemy throughout the patrol. Nine drifting mines were sighted, four of which were destroyed. Award of the Submarine Combat Insignia for this patrol is authorized. The Commander Submarine Force, Pacific Fleet, congratulates the commanding officer, officers, and men of Toro on completion of a successful patrol during which valuable services were rendered our own and allied air forces.

On August 25, Van and crew were awarded two ribbons by Captain

Jim to wear for the following campaigns: American Area and Asiatic and Pacific Area. On September 15, he was awarded and authorized to wear one star in the Combat Insignia Medal for serving on board the U.S.S. Toro during her Second War Patrol from 14 July to 27 August 1945 by J.D. Grant Commander, U.S. Navy., Commanding. Also, on September 15, in accordance with ALNAV 252 Van was credited with total foreign service duty as of 15, August 1945, 6 months. Toro was awarded 1 Star/Third Fleet Operation against Japan—10 July to 15 August 1945. Captain James D. Grant was awarded the Gold Star in lieu of Second Bronze Star Medal: "For meritorious service as Commanding Officer of the U.S.S. Toro during the Second War Patrol of that vessel in the enemy Japanese-controlled waters in the vicinity of Kii Suido from July 14 to August 20, 1945. Skillfully evading enemy countermeasures on four separate occasions, Commander Grant rescued six downed aviators and returned his ship safe to port."

While Toro was still in Guam preparing to leave for Midway, three officers were already preparing to decommission the Officers Club. Lt (jg). William J. Ruspino recalled a story when he, Lt (jg). Hugh S. Simcoe, and Lt (jg). Luna A. Davis went to the Officers Club to have a few drinks. Ruspino said that everyone in the club was talking about the end of the War and deactivating this and decommissioning that. The three of them decided that they would decommission the Officers Club. They took all kinds of souvenirs off the wall from the club and took it back to Toro. Later, the Shore Patrol tracked them down back in Toro. They had to return all the souvenirs that they had permanently borrowed from the club. That was the first time Captain Jim had sent all three to their quarters as punishment.

On August 21, moored as before.

At 1508 U.S.S. Perch got underway from alongside.

At 1513 Toro underway in accordance with CTG 17.10 OP Orders No. 21-45. Maneuvering on various courses and speeds standing out of Apra Harbor, Guam, M.I. Speed standard on two main generators 13.5 knots.

At 1538 maneuvering on various courses and speeds to gain position astern of escort (PC 813).

At 1555 commenced zigzag using arma course clock cam No. 22 on base course 320 T and pgc, in position astern of (PC 813) with U.S.S. Perch (SS313) and U.S.S. Peto (SS265) astern.

On August 22, underway on surface on course 018 T and pgc, in company with U.S.S. Perch (SS313) and U.S.S. Peto (SS265).

At 0248 exchanged recognition signals and calls with U.S.S. Mellena (AKA 32).

At 0255 exchanged recognition signals and calls with U.S.S. Robert Keller (DE 419).

At 1015 sighted land bearing 069 T distance 50 miles, Alamagan Island.

At 1125 sighted land bearing 100 T and pgc, distance 30 miles, Guguan Island.

At 1510 sighted submarine bearing 035 T, distance 8 miles.

At 1517 exchanged calls with U.S.S. Crevalle (SS291).

From August 23-27, Toro underway as before with Perch and Peto submarines enroute to Midway. Bruckel said that Toro still proceeded to Midway with caution even though the hostilities were over. They were all aware of the USS Kete submarine sunk in March 1945 between Okinawa and Midway.

On August 27, at 1320, tower on Midway Island sighted bearing 070 T.

At 1437 Lieut (jg)., H.H. Thompson, USN., came aboard as harbor pilot.

At 1440 passed No. 1 buoy abeam to port distance 30 yards, maneuvering on various courses and speeds conforming to channel. At 1459 moored starboard side to Pier S-7, Midway

island. Ships present: various units of U.S. Fleet.
At 1745 commenced taking off torpedoes and completed removal at 2015.

From August 28-September 2, Toro completed a modified refit during past seven days while moored starboard side to Pier S-7, at Midway, H.I. On August 28, at 0840 Browning, C.M., EM3c (Electrician's Mate Third Class), 570 33 88, received deep gash on left shin; while carrying laundry thru after battery, he fell into an open storeroom hatch. Treated by PhM (Doc), and by Submarine Base Sick Bay, Midway, H.I.

On September 2, at 0905 Captain D.C. MacMillan, U.S.N. came aboard and conducted readiness for sea inspection. Inspection completed at 0945. At 1115 commenced loading torpedoes and completed at 1700. Ed Hary said that he learned that his mother had passed away the week before while on Midway. He got his discharge papers before he left. He said, "I tried to get passage on any transportation faster than eight knots normal surface speed but had to ride Toro all the way to Pier 92, New York City, caught a train to Camp Wallace, Texas where I was discharged October 10, 1945."

On September 3-4, made preparations for getting underway. On September 4, at 1220, twenty-one USN passengers came aboard. At 1330 underway in accordance with C.T.G. 17.5 operation order 48-45; maneuvering on various courses and speeds conforming to channel at Midway, H.I.

At 1352 set course 180 T and pgc.
At 2207 changed course to avoid contact picked up by radar.
At 2218 resumed base course 134 T and pgc.

Swimming in Gatun Lake, Panama Canal

Enroute to Pearl Harbor

From September 5-8, underway on surface enroute to Pearl Harbor.

On September 8, at 0140 land contact on radar bearing 0005 T distance 110,000 yards.

At 0608 changed speed to standard on four main generators, 17 knots. Maneuvering at various courses and speeds conforming to Pearl Harbor Channel.

At 0938 moored starboard side to Pier 7, Submarine Base, Pearl Harbor, T.H.

At 1100, the twenty-one USN passengers left the ship.

At 1105 commenced removing torpedoes.

At 1205 commenced fueling the ship. At 1700 secured from removing torpedoes from ship and at 1740 completed fueling ship.

Shreve remembered a story about Chief Fritz "Snake" Roberts, CMoMM from Ruth, Mississippi. "Snake was quite the ladies' man and sported an Errol Flynn type mustache. Shreve said he was a very knowledgeable and efficient officer who did his job well. Soon after Toro arrived for a two-day layover in Pearl on the way back to the states, Snake was granted liberty and decided to have a few drinks before he left the ship. Meanwhile, "Uncle Charlie" (Rear Admiral Charles A. Lockwood), was on deck talking with Captain Jim when they both heard a noise as the after-torpedo room hatch opened and out popped Snake decked out in his khaki Chief's uniform. Snake looks around but then walks off the deck into the water below. (Unfortunately, he was totally drunk and fortunately his fellow shipmates fished him out)." Captain Jim turned back and said to Uncle Charlie, "did you see anything?" Uncle Charlie said, "no I didn't see anything." Both shaking their heads and laughing. Knowing what these boys went through, they were willing to cut them some slack. That's the kind of men these two were.

On September 9, Toro moored starboard side to Pier 7, U.S. Submarine Base, Pearl Harbor, T.H.

At 0800 mustered the crew at quarters, no absentees.

At 0805 inspected magazine and smokeless powder samples, conditions normal.
At 0935 underway from alongside Pier S-7, Submarine Base, Pearl Harbor, T.H., maneuvering on various courses and speeds leaving harbor.
At 0935 steadied on course 153 T and pgc, speed standard on two main generators in company with U.S.S. Blackfish (SS221) and U.S.S. Grouper (SS214).
At 1338 changed course to 080 T and pgc; released escort (PC 1078).

From September 10-14, Toro underway on course 096 T and pgc. Speed standard on two main generators, 13 knots. In company with U.S.S. Blackfish and U.S.S. Grouper submarines enroute for the Panama Canal Zone.

On September 14, at 0910 Toro maneuvering on various courses and speeds to exchange movies with U.S.S. Grouper.
At 1025 speed one third while U.S.S. Grouper and U.S.S. Blackfish exchange movies.
At 1110 exchange of movies completed.
At 1115 Toro set course for 103 T and pgc, speed standard on three main generators.

From September 15-19, Toro underway in company with U.S.S. Grouper and U.S.S. Blackfish on course 106 T and pgc. Speed standard on two main generators, 13 knots. On September 19, at 1031 Toro commenced maneuvering at various courses and speeds to exchange movies with U.S.S. Grouper. At 1112 completed exchanging movies, set course 102 T and pgc, speed standard on two main generators.

From September 20-23, Toro underway with U.S.S. Blackfish and U.S.S. Grouper enroute to Balboa, C.Z. (Panama Canal Zone). On September 23, at 0316 radar contact on land bearing 032 T and pgc, distance 35 miles, Point Burica, Republic of Panama.

On September 24, Toro underway on the surface in company with U.S.S. Blackfish and U.S.S. Grouper.

At 0202 Cape Mala Light sighted. At 0645 commenced maneuvering at various courses and speeds entering Balboa Harbor, C.Z.
At 0802 passed buoy No. 2 abeam to starboard, 125 yards, entered Panama Canal.
At 0824 passed through nets (used to protect the canal against enemy ships and submarines from entering the canal), entering Balboa Harbor, C.Z. (On the western or Pacific side of the Panama Canal).
At 0846 Toro moored port side to Pier No. 2, Submarine Base, Balboa, C.Z.
At 0902 U.S.S. Blackfish moored port side to our starboard side.
At 0925 U.S.S. Grouper moored port side to starboard side of U.S.S. Blackfish.
At 1100 Toro commenced receiving fuel from the dock. At 1830 Toro secured receiving fuel from the dock. Total fuel received 51,000 gallons.

On September 25, at 0910 U.S.S. Jack (SS259) and U.S.S. Pogy (SS266) moored astern to Pier 2, Submarine Base.

On September 26, at 0915 pilot Smith came aboard.
At 0927 Toro underway.
At 0930 maneuvering at various courses and speeds making transit of canal.
At 1025 entered Miraflores Lock.
At 1105 completed transit of Miraflores Lock.
At 1210 Toro entered Pedro Miguel Locks.
At 1240 completed transit of Pedro Miguel Locks. Commenced maneuvering on various courses at various speeds through Panama Canal channels and Gatun Lake.
At 1500 Toro anchored in Gatun Lake, anchorage with 42 fathoms of chain out on deck anchor. Anderberg took many pictures of shipmates swimming off the bow planes while Toro was anchored in Gatun Lake waiting it's turn for passage through the last and final Gatun Locks. There are also pictures of Stewart, Cook, and Russell with fishing lines out from the aft deck of Toro.
At 1850 Toro entered upper Gatun Lock.

At 1942 completed transit of Gatun Locks maneuvering on various courses and speeds conforming to channel.
At 2032 pilot Smith left the ship.
At 2044 passed through the breakwater nets on the Caribbean side of the canal and set course 003 T, and 002 pgc, speed standard on two main generators.
At 2115 U.S.S. Grouper and U.S.S. Blackfish joined company.

From September 27-28, Toro underway on course 029 T, and 028 pgc, in company with U.S.S. Grouper and U.S.S. Blackfish, speed standard on three main generators, 16 knots.

On September 28, 0855 sighted land bearing 030 T, distance 20 miles: Navassa.
At 0910 sighted land; Haiti, bearing 075 T, distance 45 miles.
At 2040 radar contact on land bearing 046 T, distance 12 ½ miles. Inagua Island.
At 2345 sighted light on Hogshy Island bearing 045 T, distance 10 miles.

From September 29-30, Toro underway on surface 001 T, 000 pgc, in company with U.S.S. Grouper and U.S.S. Blackfish. Speed standard on three main generators, 15.5 knots. At 1020 U.S.S. Grouper parted company for New London, Conn. Submarine Base.

Staten Island, New York

From October 1-2, Toro underway on surface on course 358 T and 357 pgc, in company with U.S.S. Blackfish.

On October 2, at 0655 commenced maneuvering on various courses and speeds entering New York City Channel.

At 0711 pilot Sullivan, U.S.C.G. came aboard.

At 0735 passed Gading channel buoy abeam to port 100 yards.

At 0830 moored starboard side to port side of U.S.S. Hoe at Pier #9, U.S. Naval Frontier Base, Tompkinsville, Staten Island, New York.

At 0837 pilot Sullivan, U.S.C.G. left the ship.

At 0900 U.S.S. Blackfish moored outboard of Toro.

In April 1998, I wrote to Vincent Bellezza MoMM3c, Motor Machinist Mate Third Class, from Staten Island, New York, and I heard that he had passed away on July 1, 1996, from his widow, Marie Bellezza. The couple were already married at the time Toro docked that day in 1945, at Staten Island. Marie explained to me that they had attended together, Toro's 50th Anniversary Reunion in Portsmouth, New Hampshire in 1994. She further said in her letter, "one of "Vini's" highlights was coming home from the Pacific after it was all over and hearing the announcement, "proceed to Staten Island, N.Y.," and they landed right here, down where the NYC ferry comes in from crossing the bay from Manhattan. Time passes quickly but their memories never dimmed about their experience on the "Toro" in the Pacific." She also said that she remembers him mentioning Van Auken and I'm sure they knew each other. (They were both part of the "Black Gang" or engineering gang).

On October 3, Toro moored at Pier #9, Staten Island, N.Y. At 1000 the following men were transferred to Pier 92, Third Naval District: Guttormsen, Hary, Milas, Smith, and Tate.

From October 4-9 Toro moored at Pier #9, Staten Island, N.Y. On October 4, at 0043 Commander J.D. Grant, (70273), U.S. Navy left ship on twenty (20) days leave. On October 9, at 1610 Rear Admiral C.W. Styer, U.S. Navy, ComSubLant, came aboard to make informal inspection. At 1635 Rear Admiral C.W. Styer, U.S. Navy, ComSubLant, left the ship.

From October 10-18, Toro was moored at Pier #9, Staten Island, N.Y. On October 10, Van left Toro on liberty and was the Best Man at my Uncle Baldy's and Aunt Peggy's wedding in Clinton, New York. (Dad's sister). Uncle Baldy was a submariner and together he and Dad both wore their Navy dress blue uniforms to the wedding (both right forearms proudly displaying the white twin dolphin submarine qualifying insignia on their uniforms) to the wedding. (I have a picture of them together). As part of a Navy marketing campaign, Toro and many ships around the greater New York Area conducted open houses of their ships and were open to the public. On October 18, at 1300 commenced general visiting hours and it ended at 1630.

From October 19-24, Toro was moored at Pier #9, Staten Island, N.Y., and conducted open house to the public for touring. On October 19, they had 61 visitors, October 20, 240 visitors, October 21, 850 visitors, and October 22, 550 visitors. No visitors on October 23. On October 24, at 0800 inspected magazine and smokeless powder samples, conditions normal.

At 0845 mustered crew at quarters; no unauthorized absentees.

At 1105 underway; maneuvering at various courses and speeds leaving Ambrose Channel.

At 1145 passed Romer Shoal Light abeam to starboard, distance 1000 yards.

At 1226 passed Ambrose Lightship abeam to port, distance 500 yards. Set course 140 T and pgc., and speed standard on two main generators.

At 1425 changed course to 201 T and pgc. enroute to Newport News, Virginia.

On October 25, at 0913 passed #2 buoy abeam to starboard 200 yards. At 0940 changed course to 260 T and pgc.

At 1017 pilot Wood, Lieut-Comdr., U.S.C.G.R., came aboard.

At 1018 maneuvering on various courses and speeds entering channel to Newport News, Virginia.

At 1208 moored starboard side to C. & O. Pier #3 inshore, Newport News, Virginia.

At 1209 pilot Lieut-Comdr. Wood left the ship.

USS TORO HOME WARD BOUND FROM
JAPAN

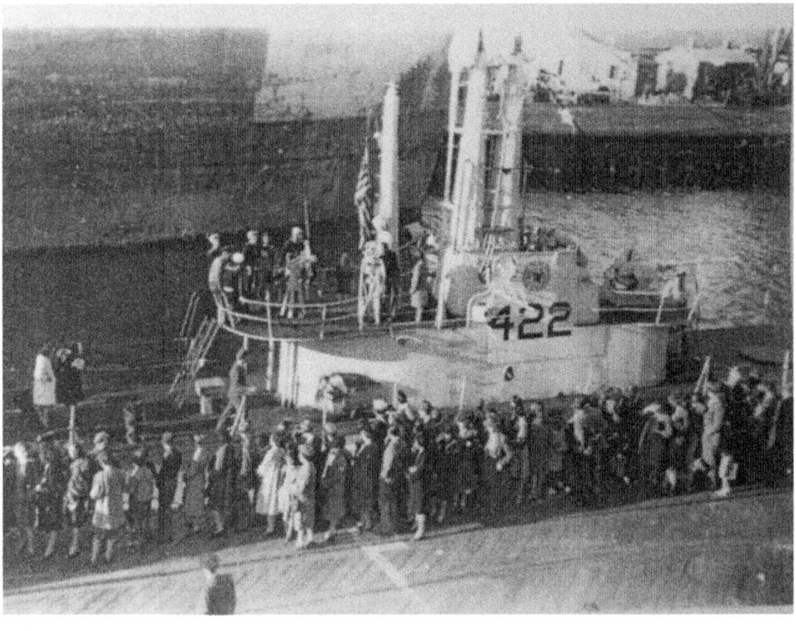

At Newport News, 1945

Newport News, Virginia

On October 26-29, Toro moored starboard side to inner berth, C. & O. Pier #3, Newport News, Virginia. Ships present destroyer U.S.S. Ellison and destroyer transport U.S.S. Upham. October 27 was established in 1922 as Navy Day by the Navy League of the United States. It marks the birthday of President Theodore Roosevelt who fathered the growth of American sea power and observes the anniversary of the introduction of the first naval bill into the Continental Congress in the year 1775, which established the U.S. Navy. A total of 375 U.S. Navy Ships of the Atlantic Fleet put into Eastern Seaboard and inland ports for Navy Day ceremonies October 27, 1945. Long before the gates were opened at 10:00 A.M., crowds of loyal and proud Americans gathered waiting to see the three ships (Toro, Ellison and Upham), at Pier #3, representative of the biggest and most powerful Navy in the world.

On Friday October 26, public tours were from 1300 to 1645.

On Saturday October 27 there were 875 visitors that toured Toro.

On Sunday October 27, there were 1000 visitors that toured Toro during the day and on Monday October 29, there were 450 visitors.

Anderberg again captured the Navy Day Event with his camera. His pictures show the proud crew of Toro in their Navy dress blue uniforms and white hats smiling and greeting the public for Toro's public inspection. Toro (the mascot) also had a short liberty and some of the crew took him to the beach at Newport News. He was on deck when the visitors began piling aboard for tours of the submersible. But Toro's attitude plainly indicated he was a seafaring dog and not interested in landlubbers-polite but disinterested. Toro will be on sick leave during the next 28 days in November to have a tumor removed from his leg at the University of Pennsylvania Veterinary Hospital in Philadelphia and will be recuperating at the home of Mrs. Mary Smith, 1007 Belmont Avenue, Philadelphia, Pa. She is the Aunt of Yeoman 1/c, Joseph Freas a member of Toro's crew.

On October 30, moored port side to Chesapeake and Ohio Pier #3, Newport News, Virginia. Ships present: various units of the U.S. Fleet.

At 1430 mustered crew at quarters, no absentees.

At 1454 pilot J.J. Peak Jr., Lieut-Comdr., came aboard.

At 1457 underway on two main generators, maneuvering on various courses and speeds leaving Newport News, Virginia enroute to Philadelphia Navy Yard.

On October 31, underway on surface making standard speed on one main generator, 11 knots; course 013 T and pgc.

At 0040 sighted Winter Shoal Light bearing 330 T, range about 12 miles.

At 0143 Winter Shoal Light abeam to port.

At 0715 pilot J.P. Johnson, U.S.C.G. came aboard.

At 1153 stationed the maneuvering watch.

At 1217 tied up port side to pier at U.S.N. Ammunition Depot, Fort Mifflin.

At 1225 Pilot Johnson left the ship. Commenced unloading 91 rounds of 5", 530 rounds 40mm, 2,640 rounds 20mm and various amounts of small arms ammunition and pyrotechnics.

At 1330 completed unloading ammunition.

At 1434 underway on two main generators and maneuvering at various speeds and on various courses into Navy Yard, Philadelphia, Pa.

At 1510 moored portside to U.S.S. Cavalla at Pier D, Navy Yard, Philadelphia, Pa.

On November 1, moored port side to starboard side of U.S.S. Cavalla, Pier D, Navy Yard, Philadelphia, Pa. Ships present, various units of U.S. Fleet. At 0900 held quarters for muster. No unauthorized absentees. Commenced removing all personal gear from the ship in preparation for overhaul and inactivation. When I met with Logsdon in December 1999, he presented me with a USN fork and dinner knife from Toro that was part of the removal of gear. He also said that everything was being mothballed. The engines were filled with Cosmoline and other preservatives. The batteries were all removed according to what Simcoe told me. Even the deck guns were put in cocoons and covered with tarps.

From November 2-January 11, 1946, Toro remained at Pier D, at the Philadelphia Naval Base, Philadelphia, Pa. Van was on leave from December 1-December 27, 1945 and returned home to New Hartford, New York to spend his first Christmas with his family since 1942, the year before he enlisted. He then returned to Philadelphia and Toro on December 27. From December 25-27, Toro was in the #1 Marine Railway Naval Base Philadelphia, Pa. On December 27, Toro was towed to Pier D, Naval Base Philadelphia, PA. On this same day Commander Grant received his orders from the Chief of Naval Personnel and they read, "Change of Duty. When directed by the Commander, Submarine Division EIGHTY-TWO, on or about 5 January 1946, you will regard yourself detached from duty as Commanding Officer, U.S.S. TORO SS-422 and from such other duty as may have been assigned you; will report to the Commander Submarine Squadron TEN for duty as Commander, Submarine Division 102 and on board a submarine of that division."

On Tuesday January 1, 1946, a poem was written by R.B. Poage Executive Officer, who was the Officer-In-Charge during the 0-4 watch. This was a Navy Tradition to write a poem about the ship on New Year's Day. It read as follows:

This ship is moored starboard side to
A sister sub the Cabrilla to you.
It's the Philly Naval Base Pier D
Westside outboard. The draft to be
Thirteen four aft, thirteen two for'ard
All ships present have severance toward
The U.S. Commander-in-Chief.

We're out of drydock five days ago
And being preserved by our own men of yeo-
man trials and many tribulations
Who send you now their plicitations
For a Happy New Year and a possible chance
To change Snafu or Fubar to a peacetime dance.

In other words,

Moored starboard side to portside U.S.S. Cabrilla westside of Pier D, Naval Base, Philadelphia, Pa. Ships present: various units of the U.S. Fleet. At 0800 mustered crew at quarters, no absentees. The following men were detached from Toro and sent to the Separation Center for demobilization in accordance with ALNAV 442-45: Bradley, Kirby, Laughlin, Tew, and Toups. As some of the guys left Toro, they were given a bottle of booze left over from the many they had stored in Toro during her active duty in the Pacific according to Logsdon.

Newport News, VA
October 1945

Separation and Demobilization

On January 3, at 1300 the following men were detached and sent to the Separation Center for demobilization in accordance with ALNAV 442-45: Rush, Neidlinger, Luoma, and Hansen.

On January 4, at 0730 detached the following men in accordance with ComSubLant dispatch 292213 of 29 December 1944: Lewis, Baldwin, Epple, Fisher, Freeman, Hall, Hay, Helm, Hixon, Ihlendorf, Jones, Keith, Maezes, McCay, Moody, Nicodemus, Pendergrass, Roth, Seegraves, Shepard, Shreve, Silagyi, Stiles. Shreve said that when he left Toro for the final time, as he was walking to the forward deck topside to exit from Toro's bullnose, he turned one last time and noticed that Toro the mascot dog was following him and was wining at him as he was leaving.

At 0800 mustered crew at quarters, no unauthorized absentees.

At 0800 detached Lieutenant John H. Cozzens, U.S.N.R. in accordance with ALNAV 344-45, for demobilization.

At 1330 oil barge (YO15) came alongside, commenced fueling ship. Received 62,650 gallons. Simcoe told me that the crew had arranged to draw lots to see who would win Toro the Mascot in a drawing to take home with him. Simcoe told me that he rigged the drawing because he wanted the dog to go to someone who lived on a farm. Bob Carlson was the one who won Toro to take home. Toro lived until 1953 with the Carlson family. It was also learned later that Moody rode a motorcycle and died in an accident on his way home from the war.

From January 6-11, Toro moored as before at Pier D. On January 11, at 0740 ATR 67 (tugboat) came along side to port; commenced preparing for being towed.

At 0910 Toro underway being towed by ATR 67.

At 0950 ATR 67 pulled ahead and attempted a long tow.

At 1030 ATR 67 anchored opposite Fort Mifflin and proceeded to put lines across to tow abreast.
At 1151 ATR 67 weighed anchor, got underway being towed abreast. At 1455 passed Pea Patch Island abeam to starboard.
At 2015 towing cables and lines parted when swells from a ship that passed to port hit the tug. Main towing cable undamaged.
ATR 67 pulled ahead and commenced long tow.

On January 12, Toro underway in tow of ATR67, proceeding to New London, Conn.
At 0510 passed Five Fathom Lightship abeam to port.
At 1422 passed Barnegat Lightship abeam to port; ATR67 changed course to 032 T.

On January 13, underway in tow of ATR67, proceeding from Philadelphia, Pa. To New London, Conn.
At 0245 passed Shinnecock Light abeam to port.
At 1305 Race Rock Light abeam to starboard.
At 1500 ATR67 anchored in New London Harbor and commenced preparations for towing abreast. Main towing cable fouled under rudder and screw of tug.
At 1515 underway from alongside of ATR67 in tow of YTL 438 and YTL 479.
At 1802 moored port side to starboard side of U.S.S. Quillback (SS424) at Victory Yard, Electric Boat Company, Groton, Conn.
At 1806 secured underway watch and released tugs.

On January 14, moored starboard side to port side of U.S.S. Quillback (SS424) at Victory Yard, Electric Boat Company, Groton, Conn. Ships present; various units of the U.S. Fleet.
At 0945 YTB 364 came alongside.
At 1000, underway up channel to Sub-Base in tow of YTB 364, tug YTB 174 following.
At 1150 Tug YTL came alongside to assist in docking.
At 1158 moored to starboard side to north side of Pier 14, U.S. Submarine Base, New London, Conn.
At 1207 secured underway watch and released tugs.

From January 15-16, Toro moored as before. On January 16, at 0815 YTB 364 came alongside.

At 0820 underway in tow by tug, for shifting berths.

At 0900 moored starboard to north side of Pier #3 Submarine Base, New London, Conn.

At 1305 received lighting and power from pier. At 1830 torpedo tube #9 leaking.

At 2330 secured leak.

From January 17 to February 6, the crew worked on Toro to prepare her to be mothballed. Each day at 0800 mustered crew at quarters, no unauthorized absentees.

On February 7, 1946, Toro moored starboard side to north side of Pier #3, U.S. Submarine Base, New London, Conn. Ships present various units of the U.S. Fleet. S.O.P.A. ComSubLant aboard U.S.S. Quillback (SS424).

At 1335 U.S.S. Toro decommissioned in compliance with ComN.L. Group 16th Fleet Ltr. P16-4/00, Serial 620 of 5 February 1946. A Decommissioning Ceremony memo from the Commander New London Group Sixteenth Fleet (Captain Wakeman B. Thorp), was sent to The Commanding Officer, U.S.S. Toro (SS422), (Captain James D. Grant), and it read as follows: The U.S.S. Toro will be placed "Out of Commission, in Reserve" on Thursday, 7 February, 1946, at 1330. Officers and crew will assemble aft of the conning tower. The men will be massed in ranks of six facing forward. The ship's officers will be in one rank on the port side facing inboard. Uniform: Officers-Service dress blue, able (with grey gloves, overcoats or raincoats). C.P.O.-Undress blue, able (with blue gloves and overcoats). Enlisted men-Dress blue, able (with blue gloves and overcoats. The Commanding Officer, U.S.S. Toro will be on board. Commander New London Group, Sixteenth arrives with officers of his staff. Commanding Officer, U.S.S. Toro reads orders. Commanding Officer (Captain Jim), directs O.O.D. to haul down commission pennant and colors (Anderberg). Bugler sounds retreat. Men who hauled down colors and commission pennant double time and present them to the Commanding Officer. Commander New London Group, Sixteenth

Fleet accepts the ship. Officer-in-Charge, U.S.S. Toro reads temporary additional duty orders to staff, New London Group as Officer-in-Charge, U.S.S. "out of commission, in reserve." Commander New London Group, Sixteenth Fleet and staff leave the ship. Captain Grant was detached in February 1946, when he was designated Commander Submarine Division 42. The Decommissioning List of the crew is at the end of this story.

Also, on February 7, 1946, Van was authorized to wear two stars in the Asiatic and Pacific Ribbon and authorized to wear the victory ribbon by J.D. Grant Commander, U.S. Navy, Commanding. On this day Van was transferred to ComSubLant FFA. Auth: NewLonGrp Ltr. P16-3/MM, Serial P-221 of 2/6/46. On February 12, 1946, Van's status changed this date to S/M Base, New London, Conn. for duty. Auth: ComSubForLant Serial P-30. Van's record also showed that he was now an Electrician's Mate Second Class, EM2c. Van stayed on at the U.S. Submarine Base, New London, Conn. until he was sent to the U.S.N. Personnel Separation Center at Lido Beach, Long Island, New York, where he was Honorably Discharged on June 27, 1946. Dad's Navy medical records showed that he grew from 69" to 70"in height, his weight increased from 140 to 145 lb. And his coat size went from 36 to 40.

July 4, 1946, Independence Day. Dad was back home in New Hartford, New York with his family. He was already enrolled in New Hartford High Summer School starting his Senior year where he met my mother Ellen (Sherman) Van Auken. Dad still had to finish his Senior year of High School as he had enlisted in the Navy after completing his Junior year. (After graduating from High School Dad went on to college. Thanks to the GI Bill of Rights, Dad could enjoy four years of college at the school of his choice. He chose Syracuse University, and in June 1950, he graduated with an electrical engineering degree).

Meanwhile, the village of New Hartford held a "Welcome Home Day" celebration for New Hartford's 1,100 service men and women. More than 5,500 people lined the decorated red, white, and blue streets in New Hartford to view the parade. A picture of the parade appeared in the Utica Observer Newspaper that day and showed the more than 100 uniformed veterans marching in the parade up Genesee Street past

Frank Moran's Texaco Station where Dad was working before he enlisted. The honorable Thomas E. Dewey, Governor of the State of New York, spoke at the celebration. He declared that "Independence Day was a time for the American people to rededicate themselves to the principles of freedom." Speaking without text or notes to the audience, the Governor said, "there was confusion all over the world today as to the meaning of democracy, the meaning of freedom, the very meaning of liberty itself." He added, "there are those in powerful governments who now twist those words to mean totalitarian government which controls the lives and in every respect the fortunes of their citizens." He went on to declare, "free government was the most creative form of society man has ever invented." Shreve while reflecting on the War, said, "War is perhaps the most useless thing in the world, but sometimes it is inevitable."

Toro After the War

After the war, Toro remained in "mothballs" at New London until she was re-commissioned on May 13, 1947. She then reported for duty to Submarine Squadron Two, Atlantic Fleet on May 28. Under Commander R.W. Alexander, the re-commissioning crew had Toro ready for sea in only 12 days after she was pulled out of the Reserve Fleet. According to Douglas Williams who was part of her crew at the time, "she had been laid up only a little more than a year and had not been stripped for spare parts like most of those boats were in reserve. The fact that we had a top heavy crew of some 18 CPO'S and 35 First Class men made it possible." On November 28, 1947, the Navy released an aerial photo of Toro torpedoing the surrendered WWII German submarine U-530 during tests 40 miles northeast of Cape Cod. This is the only known torpedoing and sinking of a vessel by Toro.

In mid-August of 1949, Toro left Portsmouth, England, with another standard diesel-electric fleet boat, the U.S.S. Corsair (SS-435), and together they escorted the "GUPPY" (Greater Underwater Propulsion Power), snorkel subs; the U.S.S. Tusk (SS-426), and the U.S.S. Cochino (SS-345), on a cold war, hunter/killer spy mission the Navy called "Operation Kayo." It was the very first U.S. Navy cold war spy mission of its kind using submarines to spy on the Soviets. They were to operate under strict radio silence the Navy called "a simulated war patrol." The orders were that after leaving England, no one onshore would know where they were and they were to disappear. Soon after their escort duty was completed, Toro and Corsair, who had accompanied Cochino and Tusk, broke off and headed toward the edge of the Arctic ice pack on their own mission northeast of Greenland for exercises in those frigid waters. Cochino and Tusk continued on to the Soviet Union for their mission. In late January

1950, Toro joined Submarine Development Group Two and helped define submarine tactics, weapons, and equipment. The boat worked in both the Atlantic and Caribbean until July 1952, when it reported to Submarine Squadron Two at New London to be used to train future submariners. During the next 10 years, it combined these activities with training and services to ships and aircraft engaged in anti-submarine warfare exercises.

On May 20, 1954, a remarkable incident occurred forty miles east of Portland, Maine involving Toro. During antisubmarine warfare exercises, Lt. (jg) Charles O. Paddock, of Frankfort, Indiana, a 26-year old Navy pilot operating out of Brunswick Naval Air Station, scored a practice "hit" on Toro. Lt. Paddock, attached to the 6th Squadron, was flying a P2V Neptune Patrol Bomber at 225 miles per hour and was 100 feet above Toro. The only thing that Lt. Paddock could see was Toro's periscope, or "eye," extended about a foot and a half out of the water. It measured three and a quarter inches in diameter. Paddock took aim and let loose his 13-pound practice bomb. Meanwhile, on board Toro, Lt. Commander William O. Hudson II, USN, Commanding Officer of Toro, was watching Paddock's bomber through the periscope at the time. He quickly swung the periscope forward to locate the "splash" in the water but when the bomb struck the periscope square on the head, he didn't see anything. "The reason," said Commander Hudson, was that "everything went black." Astounded at such accuracy, he had the top of the periscope cut from the twisted wreckage and mounted on a plaque., suitably inscribed, to the pilot, who became the first and only Navy pilot to receive the "Order of the Busted Periscope." It has never been awarded since. The plaque is currently located in the Pensacola Naval Air Station Museum in Pensacola, Florida. (I contacted the curator of the museum in April 2002, and actually held the plaque while visiting the museum). On July 1, 1962, the Commander Submarine Force, U.S. Atlantic Fleet awarded Toro the Battle Efficiency "E" representing outstanding, operational readiness in Submarine Division Twenty-One and was redesignated auxiliary submarine (AGSS422). Shortly thereafter, on the 10th of July, she began a deployment to the Mediterranean and participated in "Operation Springboard". Toro offered simulated opposition to the front line forces of the United States Sixth Fleet. During this period the officers and crew of Toro enjoyed entertaining and educational respite from the serious business of operations, in such liberty ports as Toulon, France; Genoa, Naples, Cagliari, and Sardinia Italy; Thessaloniki, Greece; and Izmir, Turkey.

On December 20, 1962, Toro completed her 12,000th dive. As far as it is known, this is the second submarine in the world that has attained this number, U.S.S. Sarda (AGSS488) being the first. Upon surfacing for the 12,000th time, a cake cutting ceremony was conducted by the Captain, CDR. T.L. Sutton, Executive Officer, C.F. Noll, Lt. and Chief of the Boat, D.R. Penley, QMCA (SS). The youngest man on board, J.A. Hanley, SN (SS), assisted the Captain in cutting the 12,000 Dive and Surface cake. The following day she made her 12,021st and final dive of her long career. For the statistically-minded, when a submarine makes more than 10,000 dives, it is equivalent to driving an automobile more than a half million miles. Making a dive requires the coordinated efforts of about 25 men performing several evolutions. At the 10,000th dive Toro's crew would have made over a million such evolutions. Faulty performance on any of these evolutions could have caused serious casualty, even loss of the ship. When Toro dives she takes on about 300 tons of sea water and when she surfaces she blows the same 300 tons of salt water out of her ballast tanks. Figured at the 10,000th dive mark, since 1944, 3,780,000 tons of water will have passed through her ballast tanks. This would be equal to the water that flows over Niagara Falls every nine minutes (as calculated at 212,000 cubic feet per second).

On March 4, 1963, the Commanding Officer, Thomas L. Sutton, U.S.S. Toro (AGSS422), announced the decommissioning of Toro to be held on March 11, 1963. "The ceremony will take place on board at Pier Twelve (12), U.S. Naval Submarine Base New London, Groton, Connecticut, or in the event of inclement weather in Building 31. All personnel who have ever served on Toro, interested personnel, and their guests are cordially invited to attend. It is requested that guests be seated by 0950. Uniform for guests will be Service Dress Blue Bravo."

The following story was written by E. Kudla Lt.(jg) USN Gunnery Officer (member of the last wardroom crew on Toro), prior to Toro's decommissioning:

FROM TWO TO TWELVE

THE USS TORO GOT UNDERWAY ON HER OWN POWER FOR THE LAST TIME FROM SOUTH OF TWO ON MONDAY, MARCH 4. WITH HER SHEARS REMOVED, TORO GAVE THE APPEARANCE OF SOME STRANGE SUBMARINE HYBRID MOVING UPSTREAM ALONG THE ROW OF SLEEK GUPPIES LINED BOW TO THE WATERFRONT. THE GIANT CRUTCH SECURED TO THE SAIL SYMBOLIZED THE RAVAGES INFLICTED ON HER DURING THE PAST MONTH BY THE "SHOPPERS." INDEED, ALL COMPASSES WENT TO THEM, AND SO TORO RESPONDED FAITHFULLY TO RUDDER ORDERS ONLY. ONWARD SHE PLOWED, AS EASILY AS THOUGH IT WERE THE FIRST TIME SHE PARTED THE WATERS OF THE THAMES WITH HER SHARP BOW. INTO THE TURN, TWISTS APPLIED, AND SNUGLY SHE RESTS AGAINST THE NORTH SIDE OF TWELVE-TOOLIE AMIDST MEMORIES OF SEAS AND MEN, TO LIE AWAITING THE DEATH-KNELL. COINCIDENTAL, ISN'T IT? FROM PIER TWO (SECOND TO ATTAIN----) TO PIER TWELVE (TWELVE THOUSAND DIVES----).

Decommissioning Ceremony

Order of Events for the Decommissioning Ceremony U.S.S. Toro AGSS-422 on 11 March 1963:

0950 Guests in place

1000 Arrival of Official Party

1000 Commander Thomas L. Sutton (Toro) requests permission to proceed with the ceremony

1001 Invocation by Commander Henry T. Lavin, Catholic Chaplain on the base

1002 Welcoming remarks and introduction of Rear Admiral Lawson P. Ramage, Deputy Commander Submarine Force, U.S. Atlantic Fleet by Commander Thomas L. Sutton (Sutton gives presentation on the history of Toro)

1010 Remarks by Rear Admiral Lawson P. Ramage

1015 Commanding Officer Thomas L. Sutton reads decommissioning authority

1016 Commander Thomas L Sutton relays orders to accomplish

- (a) "Attention" All Hands
- (b) National Anthem
- (c) Ensign, Jack and Personal Flag of Deputy Commander Submarine Force, U.S. Atlantic Fleet hauled down to coincide with music

1020 Ex-Commanding Officer Sutton reports ship decommissioned to Commander Schmidt, Commander Submarine Flotilla TWO

1020 Commander Schmidt accepts custody with appropriate remarks

1025 Benediction by Commander Henry T. Lavin, Catholic Chaplain

1030 (a) Ex-Commanding Officer Sutton announces ceremony is completed

(b) Official Party departs, nostalgic music and Crew files off, Officers file off, the Ex-Commanding Officer Sutton is the last to leave, guests depart.

March 11, 1963 USS Toro (S.S. 422) decommissioned for the second and final time.

After Toro was decommissioned to Flotilla TWO, Commander Schmidt said it was with a great deal of pride that in 1944 he was present for the commissioning of Toro, and "today it is with a great deal of regret that I see Toro decommissioned for the last time". Also participating in the decommissioning was CWO Roy Anderberg USN of Albany, New York, Recruiting Station. Mr. Anderberg lowered the ship's ensign for the last time, repeating the same part of the ceremony performed by him when Toro was decommissioned on February 8, 1946. CWO Anderberg was a member of the original crew of Toro, reporting to the pre-commissioning detail from R-16 (SS93) submarine, in October 1944. He was attached to Toro throughout her active WWII period, staying aboard until February 8, 1946, when she was put into "mothballs." Then a Quartermaster First Class QM1c, he went to new construction and was a member of the commissioning crew of Dogfish (SS350). Anderberg wrote me in May 1993, and he said, "there was a story about me in Navy Times as being probably the only sailor to put a submarine out of commission twice. I hauled down the flag in New London when she went out of commission. I was a First Class QM and last QM on board. In 1963, I wrote the Captain

(Sutton), and told him I'd like to attend the decommissioning. He invited me and then had me haul down the flag again." On that day in 1963, Captain Sutton said at the decommissioning , "it is with heavy hearts that we bid fond farewell to Toro. For her outstanding service and her part in the defense of our country we salute and offer WELL DONE to her and to all those who went with her to sea through the years." That afternoon, Toro was towed to Philadelphia Navy Yard for scrapping.

Welcome Home Parade

July 4, 1946

New Hartford, NY

◆ ◆ EVENTS ◆ ◆

MORNING:

Parade — 10:00 A. M.

Parade Route — Form on Brookline Drive, Utica, at 10:00 A.M. West on Genesee St., south on Pearl St., west on Sherman St., north on Hartford Terrace, east on Paris Road to Genesee St., south on Oxford Road to Mill St. to Playground and then to Reviewing Stand. Music to form in front of stand.

Speaking Program — 11:30 A. M.

From reviewing stand on playground

Dinner Served to Veterans in the New Hartford High School Gymnasium

AFTERNOON:

Band Concerts

Sports

EVENING:

Block Dance — 8:30 P. M. to 11:30 P. M.

SPEAKERS' PROGRAM

National Anthem

Invocation:
REV. JOHN R. O'BRIEN

Welcome Home:
A. D. ELDRED, Mayor
ROBERT J. THOMAS, Supervisor

Introduction of Governor Thomas E. Dewey
H. H. RATHBUN
Chairman of Speakers' Committee

Address of the Day:
HON. THOMAS E. DEWEY
Governor of the State of New York

Benediction:
REV. MALCOLM SWEET

Taps

Ed Hary at Boot Camp, San Diego, 1942
On lookout off coast of Japan, 1945
80th birthday, July 16, 2002

Don Shreve

Don Shreve and Mark Van Auken
2003
Louisville, Kentucky

Toro painted as a giant sonar reflector to follow Thesher's watery grave, but order cancelled.

The author with Mary and Ed Logsdon (from Indianapolis), Fireman First Class F1c, After Engine Room. Attending Subvets WWII meeting.

The author meeting Bill Ruspino,

USS Drum Submarine Museum.

On Board the USS Drum Submarine

L to R: Mark Van Auken, Bill Ruspino, his brother, Stan Stanich (author's father-in-law).

Conclusion

In the 1960s, I grew up in a Greatest Generation, middle class, neighborhood in Elyria, Ohio. A popular game that my buddies and I would play was Army. We would divide up into sides and play as sailors and soldiers based on what our fathers' service was in WW II. At the same time, we all watched our favorite WWII shows on television which included *Combat, McHale's Navy, Hogan's Heroes, and 12 O'clock High*. When our parents would get together, I never remember them talking about their war stories because they all moved on with their lives, and besides, no man' s stories were more heroic than those of the next. In my mind, they were all heroes who paid the price for freedom.

Here are my father's neighbors whose kids I grew up and played with:

Mr. Nano, Army Air Corps
Mr. Coe, Army Air Corps, pilot B-24 Mitchel Bomber
Mr. Bendik, US Marines
Mr. Thomin, US Navy Seabees
Mr. Sprague, US Marines, Guadalcanal
Mr. Copeland, US Army, Captain
Mr. Wasserman, US Army, wounded.
Mr. Kolopos, US Marines, my elementary school gym teacher.
Mr. Rakestraw, US Navy, my high school tennis coach.
Dr. Hyatt, US Army, wounded, prisoner of war, our family dentist.
Dr. Williams, US Army, our family doctor.

As I first concluded this story on April 10, 2003, it was ironically the 40th anniversary of the loss of the submarine U.S.S. Thresher (SSN 593) with 129 fathers, brothers, sons and shipmates that rode her on her last and fatal dive. In May of that year, the Navy decided to sink another submarine in the search area so that sonar could follow her down and give a "picture" of what a submarine on the bottom looked like. By following the submarine down, to her final resting place, the Navy could learn how the local ocean currents affected a falling object the size of Thresher. The submarine selected to follow Thresher to a watery grave 8,400 feet deep was Toro. Toro was to have been used as a target for new weapons. She was instead fitted out as a giant sonar reflector, with stripes painted on her hull to help in visual identification. Preparations were made for Toro to be towed to the search area and sunk under "controlled conditions" on May 20 or 21, 1963. But suddenly the plans to sink Toro were halted according to the Navy and Toro was never sunk. Joseph Andrew Gallant was a Chief Hospitalman, was a member of Thresher's crew and went down with her. Ironically, he once served on Toro.

On April 19, 1965, a letter was sent from the Defense Surplus Sales Office at the Defense Logistics Services Center in Brooklyn, New York to the Chief of Naval Operations (Code Op-432). The letter was sent to the Department of the Navy in Washington D.C. and it stated that Toro (AGSS-422) was sold for scrap to the North American Smelting Company, Marine Terminal, Wilmington, Delaware for $27,656.00. In addition, Sarda (AGSS-488) was sold for $56,767.00

I finished this book, a tribute to my father's bravery as well as his sailing buddies on the Toro, in 2002. I shared my manuscript with survivors, but it never was officially published. During a lunch in Ohio in July 2019 with my sister, Gertrude Young, and her husband, Paul, the spark for publishing the book in this format was reignited. I hope that historical information contained within it continues to document the bravery and heroism of the crew of the Toro, and that their memory is kept alive by surviving family members, friends, and readers for years to come.

DEFENSE SURPLUS SALES OFFICE
DEFENSE LOGISTICS SERVICES CENTER
FEDERAL OFFICE BUILDING
850 THIRD AVENUE
BROOKLYN, NEW YORK 11232

MAILING ADDRESS:
P.O. DRAWER NO. 1
BUSH TERMINAL STATION
BROOKLYN, NEW YORK 11232

IN REPLY REFER TO: DSSO-BK
OC:lm
DGA-18-S-3063

19 April 1965

SUBJECT: Sale of SUBMARINES (AGSS-422) and (AGSS-488)

TO: Chief of Naval Operations
Code Op-432
Department of the Navy
Washington 25, D. C.

1. References:

a. CNO Letter Op-432/kvs, Ser 1054P43, 18 June 1964, subject: same as above.

b. CNO Letter Op-432/bt, Ser 2423P43, 14 September 1964, subject: same as above.

c. CNO Letter Op-432/bt, Ser 290P43, 29 December 1964, subject: same as above.

d. CNO Letter Op-432/bt, Ser 2261P43, 13 August 1964, subject: same as above.

e. DSSO Brooklyn Sales Invitation 18-S-65-40 opened 30 March 1965.

2. Subject vessels authorized for sale by references (a), (b), (c), and (d) and listed as Items 1 and 2 of reference (e) have been awarded to North American Smelting Company, Marine Terminal, Wilmington, Delaware as follows:

Toro	Item 1	AGSS-422	$27,656.00
Sarda	Item 2	AGSS-488	$56,767.00

RECEIVED
NAVY DEPARTMENT
MAIL & FILES BRANCH
20 1965

Reg. No.
Copy No.

W. B. GRANCHER
Chief

12732

Bibliography

USS Toro Painting by John Gromosiak, Military Artist Indianapolis, 1990.

U.S.S. Toro (SS422) Deck Logs, War Patrol Reports, Action Reports, Operational Orders, USS Colahan (DD-658), U.S. National Archives, Military Reference Branch, Washington, DC.

Still Picture Branch, National Archives and Records Administration, various Navy pictures USS Toro. College Park, Maryland.

Commissioning Party of the U.S.S. Toro December 2, 1944, invitation, party announcement and crew list, Hugh Simcoe Jr.

U.S.S. Toro (SS422) Sailing lists:

First War Patrol, William Ruspino

Second War Patrol, Charles Van Auken

Submarine Crew Qualifications list, Edward Logsdon.

Scrapbook of Charles Van Auken with Toro photographs (taken by Roy Anderberg during the War with Kodak 828 camera).

Video: The History Channel: The Silent Service, 2001.

Video: USS Toro Second War Patrol Kii Suido By Lieut (jg), Hugh S. Simcoe Jr. USN, Toro photographer from original 16 mm film.

Personnel Records and Service Records, Charles W. Van Auken, Navy Reference Branch, National Personnel Records Center, 9700 Page Avenue, St. Louis, Missouri.

Personal interviews with Toro Crew members:

Edward Logsdon, December 1999, Indianapolis, Indiana.

William Ruspino, February 2000, touring the U.S.S. Drum WWII Submarine Museum, Mobile, Alabama.

Don Shreve, February 2003, Louisville, Kentucky.

Correspondence with the following Toro Crew members since 1993:

Roy Anderberg, QM1c, Quartermaster First Class
Mrs. Vincent Bellezza (Widow of Vincent, MoMM3c, Motor Machinist Mate Third Class)
Max Browning, EM3c, Electrician's Mate Third Class
William Bruckel, Lieut (jg)., Communications Officer
Mrs. DeWitt Freeman (Widow of DeWitt, S1c, Seaman First Class)
Wilhelm Guttormsen EM2c, Electrician's Mate Second Class
Edward Hary Jr., TM1c, Torpedoman's Mate First Class
Don Kleinman, F1c, Fireman First Class
Donald Koll, GM2c, Gunner's Mate Second Class
Edward Logsdon, F1c, Fireman First Class
William Ruspino, Lieut (jg), Engineering Officer
Darrell Seegraves (Brother of Ralph, Bkr3c, Baker Third Class)
Don Shreve, GM3c, Gunner's Mate Third Class
Hugh Simcoe Jr., Lieut (jg), Assistant Engineering Officer
John Smith, CEM, Chief Electrician's Mate
John Spain, EM1c, Electrician's Mate First Class

Correspondence with 9th Bomb Group B-29 Superdumbo and Rescued Survivors of B-29 Long-Winded Avenger:

Donald Cotner (B-29 Superdumbo Flight Engineer)
Chuck Lewis (Nephew of Captain Joseph Lewis pilot B-29 Long-Winded Avenger non-survivor)
Charles Smith (Right Gunner B-29 Long-Winded Avenger survivor)
Howard Stein (Radar Operator B-29 Long-Winded Avenger survivor)
Correspondence with Ernest J. "Zeke" Zellmer Officer on the USS Cavalla (SS244) February 17, 2005, and technical assistance.

WWII Submarine Museum and Navy Web Sites:

U.S.S. Cod, Cleveland, Ohio.
U.S.S. Pampanito, San Francisco, California.
U.S.S. Duncan (DDR-874), Edward E. Conrad.

Don Shreve's Experiences on the USS Toro SS422 in World War II, by Ashley Dawson, Great Niece.

The Volunteers of Spritz's Navy.

UNITED STATES SHIP, Thresher, In Memoriam, April 10, 1963, Joseph Andrew Gallant.

Submarine Force Museum, Naval Submarine base New London, Groton, Connecticut. Wendy Gulley, Archivist. Various photographs, newspaper articles, commissioning and decommissioning information, Toro memos, and Toro history reports. Biography on Captain James D. Grant.

Portsmouth Naval Shipyard Congressional and Public Affairs Office, Walter L. Ross, various articles.

Newspaper and Magazine Articles:

The Union, Manchester, New Hampshire, December 12, 1944.

Norwich Bulletin, various articles.

Hartford Courant, various articles.

Portsmouth Periscope, various articles.

Puget Sound Navy Times

Northwest Navigator

New London Day, various articles.

Daily Press, Newport News, Virginia, various articles.

The Saturday Evening Post, July 16, 1949.

Utica Observer-Dispatch

New York Herald Tribune

Polaris Magazine, U.S. Submarine Veterans, World War II, February 1994, Don Shreve Poem, The Dive.

Poems:

The Bowplanesman's Ballad, Don Shreve, Gunner's Mate Third Class, Gm3c, 1945 in the South Pacific.

Diving Officer's Lament, Don Shreve, 1945.

The Dive, Don Shreve, 1945.

Toro, R.B. Poage, Lieutenant and Executive Officer, 1 January 1946.

From Two to Twelve, E. Kudla Lt.(jg) USN, 4 March 1963.

Various Memos:

Captain J.D. Grant memo, 19 June 1945, to H.E. Stein, Camp Dealy, Guam. Donald Cotner.

Commander Submarine Force United States Pacific Fleet, Memo June 28, 1945, Presentation of Awards, Camp Dealy Guam. Hugh Simcoe Jr.

Roy A. Anderberg CWO USN letter 11 March 1963 Toro Decommissioning Lowering Toro's Ensign for the second time.

Commander T.L. Sutton, 4 March 1963, Decommissioning Memo for USS Toro (AGSS422).

Commander J.D. Grant, 7 February 1946, Decommissioning Memo for USS Toro (SS422).

Department of the Navy, Nimitz Library, United States Naval Academy, Annapolis, Maryland. Special Collections, USNA Register of Alumni, Captain Robert B. Poage, USNA Class of 1942, Captain Edward E. Conrad USNA Class of 1938. Shipmate Obituary for James Dorr Grant, USNA Class of 1931.

Books:

United States Submarine Operations in World War II, by Theodore Roscoe.

Submarines of the US Navy, Stefan Terzibaschitsch.

The Fleet Submarine in the U.S. Navy, John D. Alden, Commander, USN (Retired).

Undersea Raiders, U.S. Submarines in World War II, Milton J. Shapiro. (Cover picture, USS Toro sinking U-530, November 27, 1947).

The Fleet Type Submarine, NavPers 1610, produced for ComSubLant by Standards and Curriculum Division, Bureau of Naval Personal.

Dictionary of American Naval Fighting Ships, Volume VII, Naval Historical Center, Department of the Navy.

Portsmouth-Built Submarines of the Portsmouth Naval Shipyard,

Richard E. Winslow III.
The Blue Jackets' Manual, 1944, United States Naval Institute, Annapolis, Maryland.
The Death of the USS Thresher, Norman Polmar.
Forged in War, The Naval-Industrial Complex and American Submarine Construction, 1940-1961.
Welcome Home Day, Village and Township of New Hartford, New York, July 4, 1946.
The New Military and Naval Dictionary, Frank Gaynor.
War Under the Pacific, Time-Life Books, Keith Wheeler.
Sink'Em All, Submarine Warfare in the Pacific, Charles A Lockwood, Vice Admiral, USN (Retired).
Take Her Deep, A Submarine Against Japan in World War II, Admiral I.J. Galatin, USN (Retired).
Submariner, The Story of Basic Training at the Navy's Famed Submarine School, Henry B. Lent.
Thunder Below, The USS Barb Revolutionizes Submarine Warfare in World War II, Admiral Eugene B. Fluckey USN (Retired).
History of the 9th Bomb Group, Brigadier General Davies, Air Sea Report No. 13. Interrogation of survivors from bailed out aircraft No. 42-63509, (Long-Winded B-29). May 23, 1945.
Shimonoseki, Superdumbo and the Submarine, Donald Cotner.
Blind Man's Bluff, The Untold Story of American Submarine Espionage, Sherry Sontag, Christopher Drew, Annette Lawrence Drew.
Silent Victory, Clay Blair Jr.
Steel Shark in the Pacific, USS Pampanito SS383, Captain Walter W. Jaffee
Submarine, Edward L. Beach
Shadow Divers, Robert Kurson

Appendixes

U.S.S. Toro (SS422)
Sailing List, First Patrol

Grant, James D.	70273	Commander	Marion Wilder Grant (wife) 249 Pleasant Street Portsmouth, NH
Conrad, Edward D.	81250	Lieut.Cmdr.	Ruthabeth K. Conrad (wife) 7401 West 48th Ave Wheatridge, CO
Poage, Robert B.	123445	Lieutenant	Frances Lodema Poage (wife) c/o Commander W. R. Pease, Port Director, Port Arthur, TX
Cozzens, Jr. John H.	161294	Lieutenant	Doris H. Cozzens (mother) 22 Sprague Road Scarsdale, NY
Bruckel, William J.	186741	Lieut (jg)	Jane Bruckel (wife) 58 Reiffs Mill Road Ambler, PA
McNeal, John D.	157037	Lieut (jg)	Helen Mabbott McNeal (wife) Boyle, KS
Ruspino, William J.	227798	Lieut (jg)	Bessie Olive Ruspino (mother) 302 Fourth Street South Crosby, MN
Simcoe, Hugh S.	355988	Ensign	Alice Simcoe (wife) 8 Read Street Fitchburg, MA
Davis, Luna A.	256170	Ensign	Mary Elizabeth Davis (wife) 123 Norwood Street Lenoir, NC
Duff, Jr. John	389524	Ensign	M. Nanette Duff (mother) 163 East 81st Street New York, NY

Allen, Donald Ralph	879 42 04	Slc.	Marretta McMillin (mother) 2819 Collier Ave. San Diego, CA
Anderberg, Roy Anthony	202 59 92	QMlc	Mary Anderberg (mother) 42 Grampian Way Boston, MA
Andre, Robert Earl	664 22 59	TM2c	Hazel Andre (mother) Kingston, WA
Baker, Blayne Stanley	564 05 50	RM2c	Janet Katz (mother) 1846 North Edgemont Los Angeles, CA
Baldwin, Arnold Raymond	872 14 33	Slc	Martin Carl Baldwin (brother) Farwell, NE
Bartholomew, William Howard	249 64 87	Flc	Frank Bolton Bartholomew (father) Box 287 R.D. # 1 Sunbury, PA
Bellezza, Vincent (n)	816 49 52	Flc	Marie Theresa Bellezza (wife) 1831 Chelsea Rd. Port Richmond, Staten Island, NY
Bracken, Francis Slayhill	382 42 60	TM2c	Marjorie Lillian Bracken (wife) 89 Sumner Street Hartford, CT
Bradley, Jr. William Palmer	600 80 52	Flc	William Palmer Bradley Sr. (father) 295 Quail Street Albany, NY
Browning, Cecil Max	570 33 88	EM3c	Rose Mae Browning (mother) 1046 Marietta Street Zanesville, OH
Carlson, Robert William	266 42 73	MoMM1c	Doris Lucille Carlson (wife) 10 Webster Ave. Metheun, MA
Choage, Frank Raymond	410 87 45	MoMM1c	Celia Choage (wife) 27 Thames Street Norwich, CT

Cook, Jr., William Henry	930 31 64	Slc	Betty Jewel Cook (sister) 512 O'Hear Ave North Charleston, SC
Davis, Hal Andrew	612 62 37	EM2c	Levina Mae Davis (wife) 240 Forest Street Springfield, OH
Dugan, Richard Addison	854 07 52	Flc	William Lawrence Dugan (father) 1145 North Keystone Chicago, IL
Dutile, Frederick Joseph	803 53 64	Flc	Rosemary Theresa Dutile (wife) Bridle Rd. R.F.D. #1 North Billerica, MA
Farr, Louis Joseph	898 30 03	SC3c	Mary Louise Farr (wife) 550 Clark Street Waverly, NY
Franklin, Harold Roger	922 00 22	Flc	Mildred Elizabeth Franklin (wife) Pocono Lake, PA
Freas, Joespeh Ware	243 83 00	Y2c	Olive C. Freas (mother) 801 Queen Street Cape May, NJ
Freeman, Jr. Dewitt Wm.	671 73 96	Slc	Estrid Thelma Freeman (mother) 1137 Elm Street Lawton, OK
Grant, Everett Louis	834 97 43	MoMM3c	Mallie Grant (mother) 703 North 25th Richmond, VA
Gresham, Allen Reed	272 64 35	TM1c	Clarice Gresham (mother) Cordova, AL
Guttormsen, Wilhelm Louis	393 55 35	EM2c	Margaret Victoria Guttormsen (mother) Route, Box 132, Oregon City, OR
Hart, Jack Miles	871 68 03	RM3c	Mary Ellen Hart (wife) Cozad, NE
Hary, Jr. Edward Morace	616 55 30	TM1c	Elizabeth Ruth Hary (wife) 2008 Echols Street Bryan, TX
Hay, Eugene Carroll	755 56 50	RM3c	Bertie May Hay (mother) 560 Morgan Street Morgantown, WV

Helm, Frederick Janner	563 63 74	SM3c	Frances Helm Starr (mother) 241 East Fulton Street Butler, PA
Henricksen, James Joseph	859 07 72	EM2c	Charles August Henricksen (father) 415 North 3rd Street Clinton, IA
Ihlendorf, Robert Joseph	855 84 52	Slc	Cecelia Ihlendorf (mother) 425 Pike Street Reading, OH
Jones, Samuel Edward	379 23 25	TM3c	Vinita Alma Jones (mother) 426 South Auburn Grass Valley, CA
Jordan, Hubert Houston	274 50 84	TM2c	Gwendlyn Jo Anne Jordan (wife) 574 West 13th Street Eugene, OR
Kirby, James Joseph	823 55 14	EM2c	Annie Kirby (mother) 58 Cross Street Westerly, RI
Koll, Donald William	300 84 11	GM2c	Clara Koll (mother) 572 North Main St. Oshkosh, WI
Langley, Allen Guy	337 27 17	McMM1c	Frances Emma Langley (wife) R.F.D. #3 Greenfield, IL
Lehenmann, Lawrence Joseph	803 12 92	EM3c	Natalie Ann Lehenmann (wife) 215 Clark Road Brookline, MA
Lawrence, Earl Richard	665 45 91	McMM2c	Eburn Floyd Lawrence (father) 1315 Figueroa Ave. Walla Walla, WA
Lippman, Henry Junior	300 29 95	Flc	Lucy Elizabeth Young (mother) 200 East Lagrande Boscobel, WI
Logsdon, Edward Eugene	293 08 17	Flc	Kenneth B. Logsdon (father) 31 West Morris Street Indianapolis, IN

Lumpkins, Robert Wayne	423 63 30	MoMM2c	Effie Marie Lumpkins (mother) 3616 Wyandotte Kansas City, MO
Lundquist, Verome Lambert	668 39 95	MoMM2c	Mable V. Lundquist (mother) 134 South Washington Street Lindsborg, KS
Luoma, Olavi (n)	201 78 93	TM2c	Etla Luoma (mother) 25 Lake Concord, NH
Mains, William Douglas	346 71 02	MoMM1c	Clara Taggart Mains (wife) 4406 West 26th Street Little Rock, AR
Majocha, Michael Stanley	808 12 39	Slc	Monica Theresa Majocha (wife) 270 High New Britain, CT
Martino, Angelo Anthony	820 91 78	MoMM3c	Anthony Martino (father) 44 Belvedere Nazareth, PA
McCay, Thomas Edmund	807 35 72	QM3c	Emma McCay (mother) 149 Woodtick Road Waterbury, CT
McNamar, Burton Dave	665 66 10	Flc	Mable Nave (mother) Route 2 – Box 13 Clarkston, WA
Michael, Harry Ervan	243 68 37	CMoMM	Anna Ruth Michael (wife) c/o Murray Miller Road #1 Berwick, PA
Moody, Steward Calhoun	896 58 21	Slc	Stewart Calhoun Moody Sr. (father) Silver Creek, MS
Morgan, James Joseph	244 17 58	Flc	Rose Morgan (mother) 6412 Glennmore Philadelphia, PA
Milas, Edward Lawrence	299 94 90	EM1c	Josephine Milas (mother) 4425 West Cortez Chicago, IL

Mullane, Nicholas Henry	214 62 95	CCS	Mary Catherine Mullane (wife) 63 Holland Ave Groton, CT
Neidlinger, Lee Martin	648 79 13	CPhM	Gertha Irene Neidlinger (wife) Apt. 85 Drake Court Apts. Omaha, NE
Oakley, Jr. Oscar Carroll	872 56 07	TM2c	Oscar Carroll Oakley Sr. (father) 370 South Jefferson Ave St. Louis, MO
Parry, David Humphrey	819 60 41	RT2c	Humphrey J. Parry (father) 299 Lehighgap Street Walnutport, PA
Pendergrass, Fred Merel	357 62 29	SC3c	W. A. Pendergrass (mother) Route #1 Gustine, TX
Rivera, Bill (n)	664 45 27	St2c	Marcelina Agcaoili (sister) 1627 Aupuni Honolulu, HI
Roberts, Fritz Fulton	274 43 61	CMoMM	Jessie Lee Roberts (mother) Ruth, MS
Saugstad, Gordon Leroy	313 42 12	EM3c	Norman Carlton Saugstad (mother) Flint, MI
Seegraves, Ralph Clifford	951 42 12	Slc	Essie Seegraves (mother) 92 Mechanic Pontiac, MI
Shepard, Jr. Marvin Osco	640 44 89	Slc	Dora Adell Shepard (mother) Vernon, TN
Shreve, Don Hafley	550 44 72	Slc	Ruth Moser Shreve (mother) 1825 West Clinch Ave Knoxville, TN
Smith, Jr. John Edward	250 51 53	CEM	Bertha Dell Smith (wife) Harbor Road, R.D. #2 New Castle, PA

Spain, John Hughes	296 11 71	EM1c	Mary Emily Spain (wife) 1242 Court Ave Memphis, TN
Sparks, Paul Mason	873 85 85	Flc	Nina Glenn Sparks (mother) 719 West 4th St. Sedolia, MO
Snyder, David William	291 44 60	CRM	Leota Ruth Snyder (wife) Kittery, ME
Stiles, Dean Farman	825 41 62	Slc	Jennie Donald Stiles (mother) Barton, VT
Strahan, Jr. John Clifford	758 59 52	Slc	Helen Strahan (mother) 140 Church Street Bridgeton, NJ
Stuart, James Alford	878 06 17	MoMM2c	Marguerite Stuart (mother) 532 West Malvern St. Fullerton, CA
Tate, Miles Claude	656 23 32	RT1c	Larraine Elizabeth Tate (wife) 1566 48th Ave. San Francisco, CA
Toups, Welton Joseph	842 34 42	Slc	Nettie Kate Toups (wife) 113 2nd, Jones Street Box 34 Pelly, TX
Tucker, Henry Bitler	816 02 35	EM3c	Evelyn Thievmann Tucker (wife) 12 Albany Rockville Centre, NY
Van Auken, Charles Willard	800 78 09	EM3c	Arthur Hammond Van Auken (father) 3 Jordan Road New Hartford, NY
Van Leuven, Franklin Augustus	224 63 20	MoMM2c	Edwina Iona Leuven (wife) 22 Delmont Street Presque Isle, ME
Wakefield, Bruce Earl	385 85 87	MoMM2c	Myrtle Wakefield (mother) 3201 41st Southwest St. Seattle, WA

Williams, George (n)	968 37 03	StM2c	Deloris Gloria Williams (wife) 1107 Genessee Houston, TX
Williams, Joseph Fredey	201 72 17	GM1c	Maria Marilyn Williams (wife) 11 Akron Roxbury 19, MA
Williams, Verner Hill	271 45 58	CSM	Gladys Elenor Williams (wife) 1122 West Brookes Ave. San Diego, CA
Zarnick, Jerome Clarence	726 99 03	Slc	Anna Zarnick (mother) 3419 North Monticello Ave Chicago, IL

U.S.S. Toro (SS422)
Sailing List, Second Patrol

Grant, James D.	70273	Commander	Marion Wilder Grant (wife) 249 Pleasant Street Portsmouth, NH
Poage, Robert B.	123445	Lieutenant	Frances Lodema Poage (wife) c/o Commander W. R. Pease, Port Director, Port Arthur, TX
Cozzens, Jr. John H.	161294	Lieutenant	Doris H. Cozzens (mother) 22 Sprague Road Scarsdale, NY
Bruckel, William J.	186741	Lieut (jg)	Jane Bruckel (wife) 58 Reiffs Mill Road Ambler, PA
McNeal, John D.	157037	Lieut (jg)	Helen Mabbott McNeal (wife) Boyle, KS
Ruspino, William J.	227798	Lieut (jg)	Bessie Olive Ruspino (mother) 302 Fourth Street South Crosby, MN
Hower, Wayne F.	298277	Lieut (jg)	Mary Hower (mother) 437 Trumbull Ave Warren, OH
Simcoe, Hugh S.	355988	Ensign	Alice Simcoe (wife) 8 Read Street Fitchburg, MA
Davis, Luna A.	256170	Ensign	Mary Elizabeth Davis (wife) 123 Norwood Street Lenoir, NC
Duff, Jr. John	389524	Ensign	M. Nanette Duff (mother) 163 East 81st Street New York, NY

Allen, Donald Ralph	879 42 04	Slc.	Marretta McMillin (mother) 2819 Collier Ave. San Diego, CA
Anderberg, Roy Anthony	202 59 92	QMlc	Mary Anderberg (mother) 42 Grampian Way Boston, MA
Andre, Robert Earl	664 22 59	TM2c	Hazel Andre (mother) Kingston, WA
Baker, Blayne Stanley	564 05 50	RM2c	Janet Katz (mother) 1846 North Edgemont Los Angeles, CA
Baldwin, Arnold Raymond	872 14 33	Slc	Martin Carl Baldwin (brother) Farwell, NE
Bartholomew, William Howard	249 64 87	Flc	Frank Bolton Bartholomew (father) Box 287 R.D. # 1 Sunbury, PA
Bellezza, Vincent (n)	816 49 52	Flc	Marie Theresa Bellezza (wife) 1831 Chelsea Rd. Port Richmond, Staten Island, NY
Bracken, Francis Slayhill	382 42 60	TM2c	Marjorie Lillian Bracken (wife) 89 Sumner Street Hartford, CT
Bradley, Jr. William Palmer	600 80 52	Flc	William Palmer Bradley Sr. (father) 295 Quail Street Albany, NY
Browning, Cecil Max	570 33 88	EM3c	Rose Mae Browning (mother) 1046 Marietta Street Zanesville, OH
Brown, Richard Carlton	600 56 88	TM2c	Carolyn Brown (mother) 236 Conklin Ave Binghamton, NY
Carlson, Robert William	266 42 73	MoMM1c	Doris Lucille Carlson (wife) 10 Webster Ave. Metheun, MA

Cassidy, George Robert	711 71 29	Slc	Richard L. Boutwell (sister) 62 Fairview Hts. Portland, CT
Cook, Jr., William Henry	930 31 64	Slc	Betty Jewel Cook (sister) 512 O'Hear Ave North Charleston, SC
De Los Santos, Julio Dahipon	582 65 48	StM3c	Maria Dantes Dahipon (mother) Subic, Zambales, Luzon, Philippine Islands
Denker, Thomas (n)	642 07 54	MoMM3c	William George Denker (father) 24 York Ave Norwich, CT
Dugan, Richard Addison	854 07 52	Flc	William Lawrence Dugan (father) 1145 North Keystone Chicago, IL
Dutile, Frederick Joseph	803 53 64	Flc	Rosemary Theresa Dutile (wife) Bridle Rd. R.F.D. #1 North Billerica, MA
Farr, Louis Joseph	898 30 03	SC3c	Mary Louise Farr (wife) 550 Clark Street Waverly, NY
Franklin, Harold Roger	922 00 22	Flc	Mildred Elizabeth Franklin (wife) Pocono Lake, PA
Freas, Joespeh Ware	243 83 00	Y2c	Olive C. Freas (mother) 801 Queen Street Cape May, NJ
Freeman, Jr. Dewitt Wm.	671 73 96	Slc	Estrid Thelma Freeman (mother) 1137 Elm Street Lawton, OK
Grant, Everett Louis	834 97 43	MoMM3c	Mallie Grant (mother) 703 North 25th Richmond, VA
Gresham, Allen Reed	272 64 35	TM1c	Clarice Gresham (mother) Cordova, AL
Guttormsen, Wilhelm Louis	393 55 35	EM2c	Margaret Victoria Guttormsen (mother) Route, Box 132, Oregon City, OR

Hart, Jack Miles	871 68 03	RM3c	Mary Ellen Hart (wife) Cozad, NE
Hary, Jr. Edward Morace	616 55 30	TM1c	Elizabeth Ruth Hary (wife) 2008 Echols Street Bryan, TX
Hay, Eugene Carroll	755 56 50	RM3c	Bertie May Hay (mother) 560 Morgan Street Morgantown, WV
Helm, Frederick Janner	563 63 74	SM3c	Frances Helm Starr (mother) 241 East Fulton Street Butler, PA
Henricksen, James Joseph	859 07 72	EM2c	Charles August Henricksen (father) 415 North 3rd Street Clinton, IA
Ihlendorf, Robert Joseph	855 84 52	Slc	Cecelia Ihlendorf (mother) 425 Pike Street Reading, OH
Jones, Samuel Edward	379 23 25	TM3c	Vinita Alma Jones (mother) 426 South Auburn Grass Valley, CA
Jordan, Hubert Houston	274 50 84	TM2c	Gwendlyn Jo Anne Jordan (wife) 574 West 13th Street Eugene, OR
Keith, Jr., Glen Floyd	383 21 68	SC3c	Glen Floyd Keith (father) 6965 Amherst St. San Diego, CA
Kirby, James Joseph	823 55 14	EM2c	Annie Kirby (mother) 58 Cross Street Westerly, RI
Kleinman, Don Walter	368 78 10	Flc	David Conrad Kleinman (father) Box 45 American Fork, UT
Koll, Donald William	300 84 11	GM2c	Clara Koll (mother) 572 North Main St. Oshkosh, WI

Laughlin, Roger Lynn	625 84 28	MoMM2c	Rosa Laughlin (mother) Box 761 Robstown, TX
Lehenmann, Lawrence Joseph	803 12 92	EM3c	Natalie Ann Lehenmann (wife) 215 Clark Road Brookline, MA
Lippman, Henry Junior	300 29 95	Flc	Lucy Elizabeth Young (mother) 200 East Lagrande Boscobel, WI
Logsdon, Edward Eugene	293 08 17	Flc	Kenneth B. Logsdon (father) 31 West Morris Street Indianapolis, IN
Lundquist, Verome Lambert	668 39 95	MoMM2c	Mable V. Lundquist (mother) 134 South Washington Street Lindsborg, KS
Luoma, Olavi (n)	201 78 93	TM2c	Etla Luoma (mother) 25 Lake Concord, NH
Mains, William Douglas	346 71 02	MoMM1c	Clara Taggart Mains (wife) 4406 West 26th Street Little Rock, AR
Majocha, Michael Stanley	808 12 39	Slc	Monica Theresa Majocha (wife) 270 High New Britain, CT
Martino, Angelo Anthony	820 91 78	MoMM3c	Anthony Martino (father) 44 Belvedere Nazareth, PA
McCay, Thomas Edmund	807 35 72	QM3c	Emma McCay (mother) 149 Woodtick Road Waterbury, CT
McNamar, Burton Dave	665 66 10	Flc	Mable Nave (mother) Route 2 – Box 13 Clarkston, WA
Michael, Harry Ervan	243 68 37	CMoMM	Anna Ruth Michael (wife) c/o Murray Miller Road #1 Berwick, PA

Milas, Edward Lawrence	299 94 90	EM1c	Josephine Milas (mother) 4425 West Cortez Chicago, IL
Moody, Steward Calhoun	896 58 21	Slc	Stewart Calhoun Moody Sr. (father) Silver Creek, MS
Morgan, James Joseph	244 17 58	Flc	Rose Morgan (mother) 6412 Glennmore Philadelphia, PA
Neidlinger, Lee Martin	648 79 13	CPhM	Gertha Irene Neidlinger (wife) Apt. 85 Drake Court Apts. Omaha, NE
Parry, David Humphrey	819 60 41	RT2c	Humphrey J. Parry (father) 299 Lehighgap Street Walnutport, PA
Pendergrass, Fred Merel	357 62 29	SC3c	W. A. Pendergrass (mother) Route #1 Gustine, TX
Rivera, Bill (n)	664 45 27	St2c	Marcelina Agcaoili (sister) 1627 Aupuni Honolulu, HI
Roberts, Fritz Fulton	274 43 61	CMoMM	Jessie Lee Roberts (mother) Ruth, MS
Russell, Vaughn Lamoine	862 24 23	MoMM2c	Edna Russell (wife) R.F.D. #1 Grand Ledge, MI
Saugstad, Gordon Leroy	313 42 12	EM3c	Norman Carlton Saugstad (mother) Flint, MI
Seegraves, Ralph Clifford	951 42 12	Slc	Essie Seegraves (mother) 92 Mechanic Pontiac, MI
Shepard, Jr. Marvin Osco	640 44 89	Slc	Dora Adell Shepard (mother) Vernon, TN
Shreve, Don Hafley	550 44 72	Slc	Ruth Moser Shreve (mother) 1825 West Clinch Ave Knoxville, TN

Smith, Jr. John Edward	250 51 53	CEM	Bertha Dell Smith (wife) Harbor Road, R.D. #2 New Castle, PA
Snyder, David William	291 44 60	CRM	Leota Ruth Snyder (wife) Kittery, ME
Spain, John Hughes	296 11 71	EM1c	Mary Emily Spain (wife) 1242 Court Ave Memphis, TN
Sparks, Paul Mason	873 85 85	Flc	Nina Glenn Sparks (mother) 719 West 4th St. Sedolia, MO
Stewart, Robert Eugene	940 79 90	Flc	Elizabeth Stewart (wife) 305 Dayton Ave Springfield, OH
Stiles, Dean Farman	825 41 62	Slc	Jennie Donald Stiles (mother) Barton, VT
Strahan, Jr. John Clifford	758 59 52	Slc	Helen Strahan (mother) 140 Church Street Bridgeton, NJ
Tate, Miles Claude	656 23 32	RT1c	Larraine Elizabeth Tate (wife) 1566 48th Ave. San Francisco, CA
Tew, Jr., Frank Fisher	836 99 76	RT1c	Alice H. Tew (wife) 1917 D Street Washington, DC
Toups, Welton Joseph	842 34 42	Slc	Nettie Kate Toups (wife) 113 2nd, Jones Street Box 34 Pelly, TX
Van Auken, Charles Willard	800 78 09	EM3c	Arthur Hammond Van Auken (father) 3 Jordan Road New Hartford, NY
Van Leuven, Franklin Augustus	224 63 20	MoMM2c	Edwina Iona Leuven (wife) 22 Delmont Street Presque Isle, ME

Wakefield, Bruce Earl	385 85 87	MoMM2c	Myrtle Wakefield (mother) 3201 41st Southwest St. Seattle, WA
Zarnick, Jerome Clarence	726 99 03	Slc	Anna Zarnick (mother) 3419 North Monticello Ave Chicago, IL
Davis, Hal Andrew	612 62 37	EM1c	Levina Mae Davis (wife) 240 Forest Street Springfield, OH

Official Log Book Records

showing commissioning list and de-commissioning list.

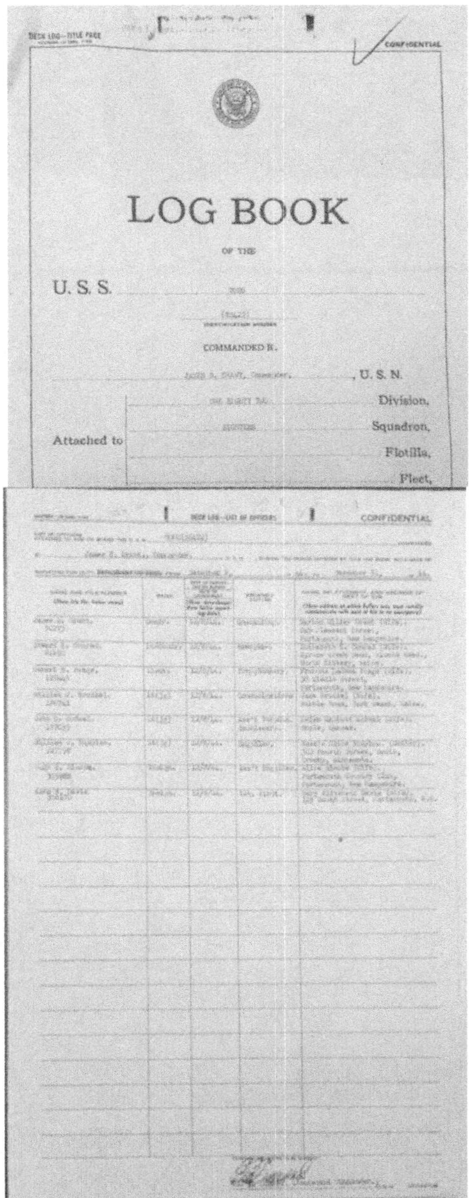

CONFIDENTIAL

LOG BOOK

OF THE

U. S. S.

COMMANDED BY

, U. S. N.

Division,

Squadron,

Attached to

Flotilla,

Fleet,

CONFIDENTIAL

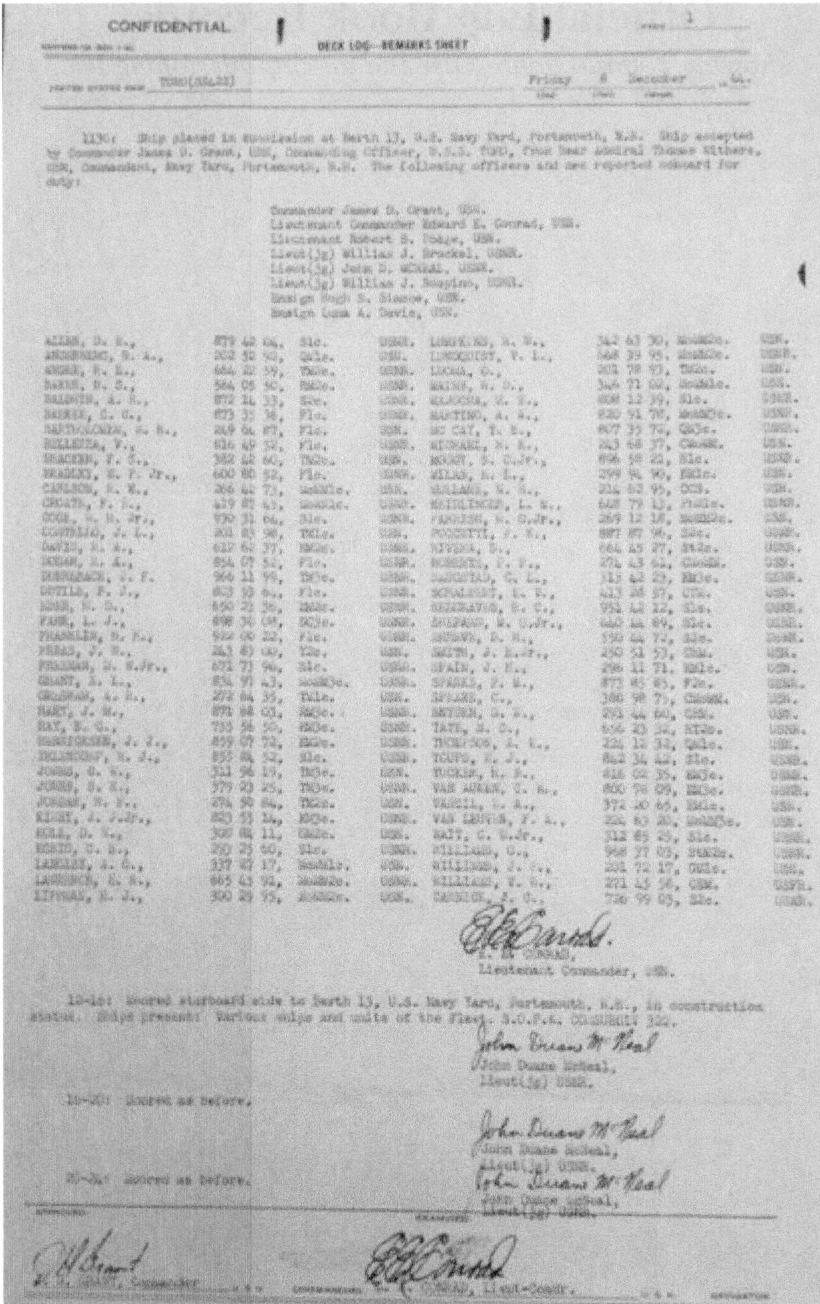

CONFIDENTIAL

DECK LOG—REMARKS SHEET

Page 1

TODD(DD-22) Friday 8 December 44.

1130: Ship placed in commission at Berth 13, U.S. Navy Yard, Portsmouth, N.H. Ship accepted by Commander James D. Grant, USN, Commanding Officer, U.S.S. TODD, from Rear Admiral Thomas Withers, USN, Commandant, Navy Yard, Portsmouth, N.H. The following officers and men reported aboard for duty:

Commander James D. Grant, USN.
Lieutenant Commander Edward E. Conrad, USN.
Lieutenant Robert S. Page, USN.
Lieut(jg) William J. Brackel, USNR.
Lieut(jg) John D. McNEAL, USNR.
Lieut(jg) William J. Bespino, USNR.
Ensign Hugh S. Slamoe, USN.
Ensign Lena A. Davis, USN.

ALLAN, D. R.,	879 42 04,	S1c.	USNR.	LINDFORS, R. W.,	342 63 30,	[illegible]	USN.
ARMSTRONG, R. A.,	202 52 90,	QM1c.	USN.	LUNDQUIST, V. L.,	568 39 95,	[illegible]	USNR.
ARNER, R. L.,	664 22 59,	TM2c.	USNR.	LUCAS, C.,	201 78 53,	TM3c.	USN.
BAKER, N. S.,	564 05 90,	RM2c.	USNR.	MAINE, W. D.,	346 71 60,	[illegible]	USN.
BALDWIN, A. R.,	872 34 33,	S2c.	USNR.	MALOOSA, W. S.,	808 12 39,	S1c.	USNR.
BARKER, C. C.,	873 35 38,	F1c.	USNR.	MARTINO, A. A.,	820 51 78,	[illegible]	USNR.
BARTHOLOMEW, W. H.,	249 04 87,	F1c.	USN.	MC CAY, T. L.,	807 35 74,	GM3c.	USNR.
BOLLETTA, V.,	616 49 52,	F1c.	USNR.	MICHAEL, H. R.,	243 68 37,	CGMA.	USN.
BRACKEN, F. S.,	382 42 60,	TM3c.	USN.	MOODY, D. C.Jr.,	896 58 21,	S1c.	USNR.
BRADLEY, W. F. Jr.,	600 80 52,	F1c.	USNR.	MILAN, A. L.,	299 94 90,	EM1c.	USN.
CARLSON, R. E.,	266 42 73,	[illegible]	USN.	WILLIAMS, W. H.,	214 63 95,	CCS.	USN.
CROATE, F. L.,	419 87 45,	[illegible]	USNR.	MEILINGER, L. W.,	668 79 13,	PhM1c.	USNR.
COOK, H. H. Jr.,	930 31 04,	S1c.	USNR.	PARRISH, W. C.Jr.,	269 12 18,	[illegible]	USN.
COSTELLO, J. L.,	201 83 98,	TM1c.	USN.	POSSETTI, F. E.,	887 87 96,	S2c.	USNR.
DAVIS, R. A.,	612 60 77,	RM3c.	USNR.	RIVERA, D.,	664 45 27,	St2c.	USNR.
DORAN, R. A.,	854 07 52,	F1c.	USNR.	ROBERTS, F. F.,	274 43 62,	CMoMM.	USN.
DORNBACH, J. F.,	960 11 99,	TM3c.	USNR.	SANDSTAD, C. L.,	313 42 23,	RM3c.	USNR.
DOTILS, F. J.,	803 30 64,	F1c.	USNR.	SCHALBERT, L. E.,	413 38 37,	CTM.	USN.
EBER, N. S.,	850 22 36,	RM2c.	USNR.	SEIGRAVES, R. C.,	951 42 12,	S1c.	USNR.
FAUK, L. J.,	898 30 08,	SC3c.	USNR.	SHEPARD, W. C.Jr.,	640 44 84,	S1c.	USNR.
FRANKLIN, H. R.,	902 00 22,	F1c.	USNR.	SHREVE, D. H.,	550 64 73,	S1c.	USNR.
FREAS, J. R.,	243 83 60,	Y2c.	USN.	SMITH, J. L.Jr.,	250 51 53,	CRM.	USN.
FRESHMAN, D. W.Jr.,	671 73 96,	S1c.	USNR.	SPAIN, J. H.,	296 11 71,	RM1c.	USN.
GRANT, R. L.,	834 97 43,	[illegible]	USNR.	SPARKS, F. B.,	877 85 85,	F2c.	USNR.
GRESHAM, A. H.,	272 84 35,	TM1c.	USN.	SPEARS, C.,	380 98 75,	CMoMM.	USN.
HART, J. M.,	871 88 03,	RM3c.	USNR.	SNYDER, D. E.,	293 44 60,	CGM.	USN.
HAY, R. G.,	733 56 50,	RM3c.	USNR.	TATE, R. D.,	656 23 32,	RT2c.	USNR.
HENRICKSEN, J. J.,	859 07 72,	RM3c.	USNR.	THOMPSON, A. L.,	224 12 32,	QM1c.	USN.
HOLLENKOPF, W. J.,	855 84 52,	S1c.	USNR.	TOUPS, R. J.,	842 34 42,	S1c.	USNR.
JONES, O. R.,	311 96 19,	TM3c.	USN.	TUCKER, R. B.,	416 08 35,	RM3c.	USNR.
JONES, R. K.,	379 23 25,	TM3c.	USNR.	VAN AUKEN, T. B.,	800 78 09,	EM3c.	USNR.
JORDAN, H. R.,	274 50 84,	TM2c.	USN.	VASSIL, L. A.,	372 20 65,	RM1c.	USN.
KIRBY, J. J.Jr.,	823 53 14,	RM3c.	USNR.	VAN LEUVEN, F. A.,	224 63 20,	[illegible]	USN.
KOLL, D. W.,	300 88 11,	GM2c.	USN.	WAIT, C. W.Jr.,	312 85 25,	S1c.	USNR.
KOSKO, S. R.,	293 23 60,	S1c.	USNR.	WILLIAMS, G.,	958 37 03,	StM2c.	USNR.
LANGLEY, A. C.,	337 47 17,	[illegible]	USN.	WILLIAMS, J. C.,	201 72 17,	GM1c.	USN.
LAWRENCE, E. R.,	665 43 91,	[illegible]	USNR.	WILLIAMS, E. W.,	271 45 56,	CBM.	USFR.
LIPPMAN, H. J.,	300 29 95,	[illegible]	USN.	ZARBICK, J. O.,	730 99 03,	S2c.	USNR.

E. E. CONRAD,
Lieutenant Commander, USN.

12-16: Moored starboard side to Berth 13, U.S. Navy Yard, Portsmouth, N.H., in construction status. Ships present: Various ships and units of the Fleet. S.O.P.A. COMSUBDIV 322.

John Duane McNeal,
Lieut(jg) USNR.

16-20: Moored as before.

John Duane McNeal,
Lieut(jg) USNR.

20-24: Moored as before.

John Duane McNeal,
Lieut(jg) USNR.

APPROVED: J. D. GRANT, Commander U.S.N. EXAMINED: E. E. CONRAD, Lieut-Comdr. U.S.N.

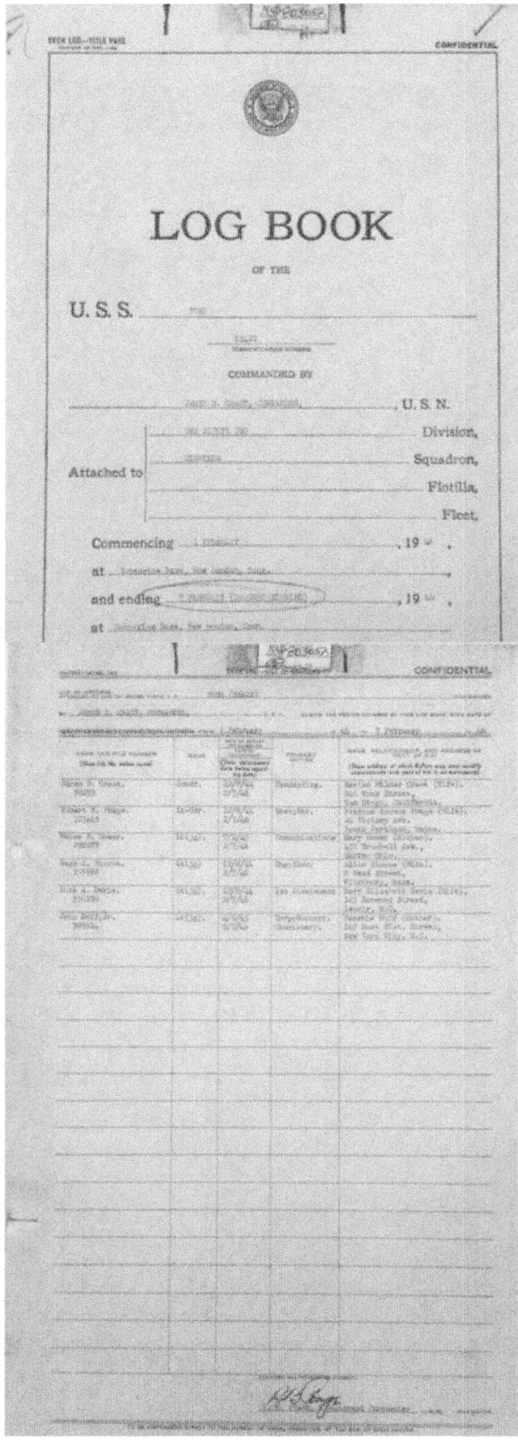

CONFIDENTIAL

LOG BOOK

OF THE

U.S.S.

COMMANDED BY

, U.S.N.

Attached to

Division,

Squadron,

Flotilla,

Fleet,

Commencing , 19 ,

at

and ending , 19 ,

at

CONFIDENTIAL

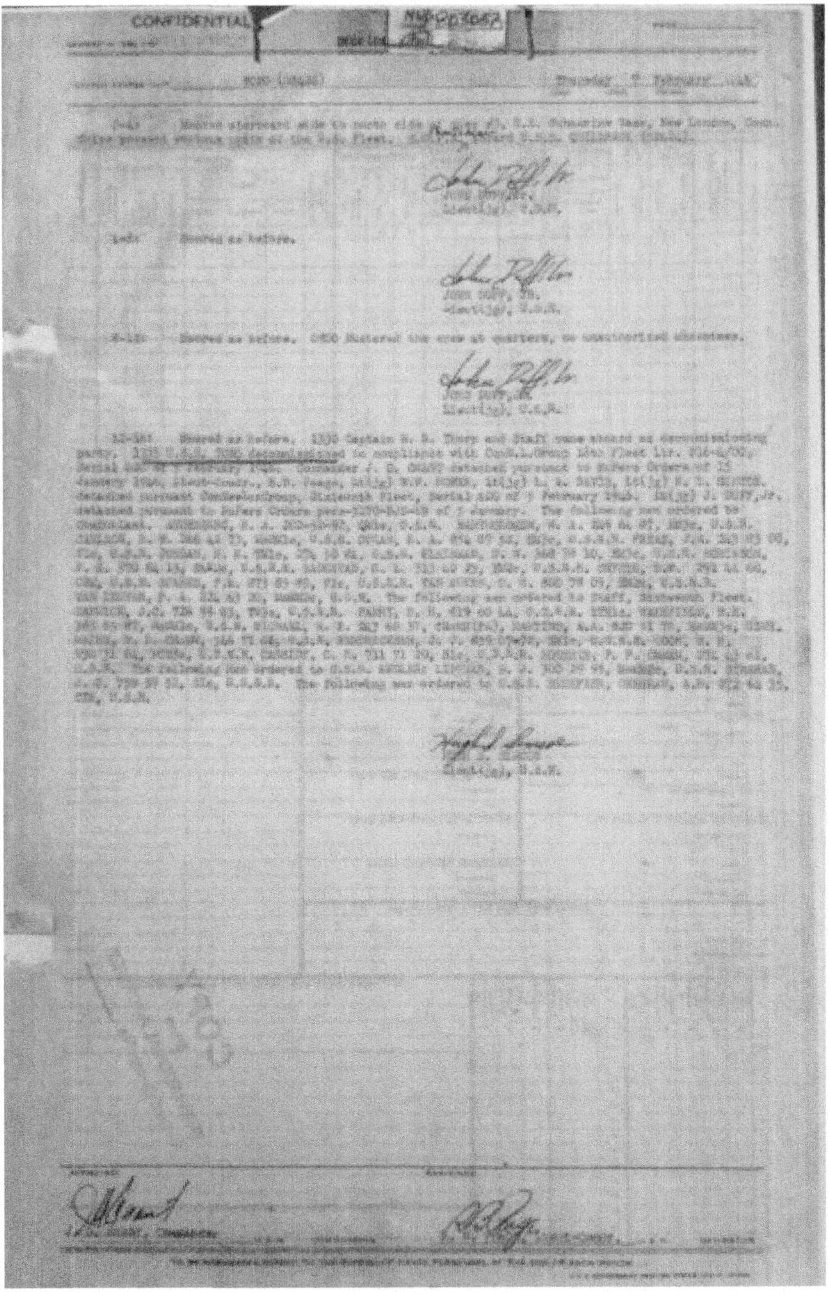
CONFIDENTIAL

Moored as before.

Moored as before. 0800 Mustered the crew at quarters, no unauthorized absentees.

From the Scrapbook of Charles W. Van Auken

WILLIAMS, MOODY, STUART, POQUE SNYDER
SHEPARD, COMMING IN AFTER FIRST
WAR PATROL

GOING HOME

TORO HOMEWARD BOUND FROM
JAPAN

MARINE RAILWAY
NEW LONDON CONN

BAKER, TATE, MCKAY

RESCUE WORK

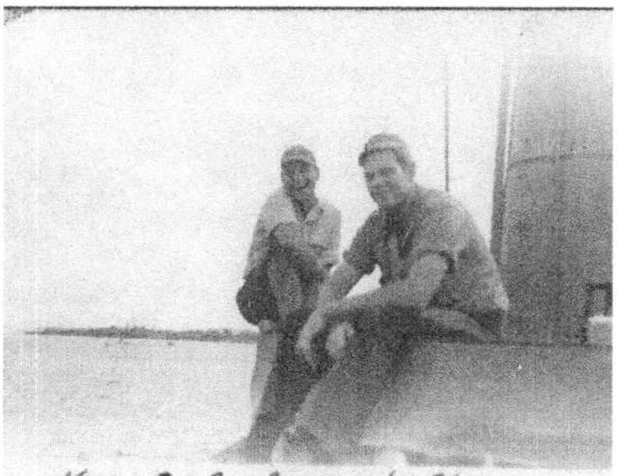

MODY QM 3/C, RASPINO LT. S.G.

STEWART P 1/c, COOK F.C 3/c

SANTOS

CAPTAIN GRANT

BROWNING. EM 1/c

MAINS, CPT. GRANT LT. JG. BRICKEL

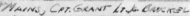

KIETH SC 3/c, APT. BAND HATCH

THE 5"26 GUN

VISITING DAY ON THE TORO

Franklin and "Van"

FRANKLYN, FARR, KLINMAN

McKAY QM 3/c

SEAGRAVES, KLINM., FRANKLYN

FRANKLYN MoMM 1/c, FARR SC 2/c & VISITOR

ANDERBERG QM 1/c

BROWNING, KIETH, FRANKLIN, ROBERTS
STILES

BAKER RM 1/c FREEMAN RM 3/c

LUNQUIST MoMM 1/c HENDRICKSON EM 2/c
SWIMMING AT GATUN LAKE, PANAMA CANAL

CONNING TOWER

ROBERTS C.MoMM, LIPPMAN MoMM 3/c

ICE OFF NEW PORT, R.I.

QUARTER MASTER TO THE BRIDGE

1. Launching tag for guests attending the ceremony (08-23-1944)
2. Deck planking (actual piece of wood from the deck of the USS Toro, (Charles Van Auken was a plank owner from construction to commissioning to decommissioning)
3. Submarine qualification pin and two stars representing each successful war patrol
4. Worn on the dress blue uniform right forearm indicating submarine service
5. Lock for personal locker aboard Toro
6. Van's Waltham Navy issue 24-hour GCT (Greenwich Civil Time) pocket watch
7. Steel-covered Bible for chest pocket
8. Van's USN personal identification bracelet
9. Van's electrician flashlight

Crew Qualifications

CREW QUALIFICATIONS - GENERAL.

1. Be able to rig ship for dive. Locate all valves and fittings on the rig for dive bills and know why each is open or closed.
2. Be able to rig all compartments for any emergency! Know the most important items on the bills and why each item is part of rigging for the emergency.
3. Make ready and fire a torpedo tube. be able to flood, blow or pump the tubes using W.R.T. and forward trim. Know what all the attachments are and their uses.
4. Start and secure an engine. (Engineers only)
5. Operate main control cubicle. (Electricians only)
6. Operate all pump room equipment. (Auxiliarymen only)
7. Make an escape from either torpdo room.
8. Grease topside. (Seamen only)
9. Tell number and locale: Oxygen bottles; fire extinguishers; CO2 absorbent; emergency lights; smoke lungs; escape lungs; lighting panels; bilge suctions.
10. Locate all tanks on the ship. Tell which tnks are outisde and under each compartment.
11. Know where all items on below decks check off list are located and why they are on the list.
12. Be able to shift fresh water tanks.
13. Make anchor ready for letting go. Operate both capstans, and know the orders pertaining to mooring or anchoring.
14. Be proficient in use of trim manifold. Be able to pump, flood or blow from or to any tank.
15. Be able to pump bilges and to cross connect trim and drain lines so as to use either pump..
16. Locate all salvage connections and explain how and why they are used.
17. Blow either MAIN sanitary or the after head.
18. Shift from rigging or tilting to capstan, fore and aft.
19. Locate all main and emergency vents. Shift main vents from power to hand or lock.
20. Locate all life belts, damage control kits, 7MC and 1MC outlets, fire bag, fire hose and nozzle and repair kit.
21. Understand the fuel system in regards to filling connections, use of compensating system, venting of expansion and safety devices and precautions.
22. Understand the main populsion equipment. Explain the sequence of events in getting power from eigines to screws. Know horsepower of engines and motors. Know make and type of engines. Shaft horsepower.
23. Know in general the hydraulic system; how to operate the plants and hydraulic manifolds; operate bow and stern planes nd steering in power, hand and emergency; rig bow planes in power and hand.
24. Line up ventilation system for ny conditions, including battery charge.
25. Know number of cells in the battery, how ventilated, in general, and safety precautions while charging.
26. Locate ll air bottles and hull stops for each.
27. Locate all battle lanterns and emergency flashlight lockers. Locate all trim line hose connections.
28. Operate all control room equipment except gyro, I.C., fathometers, radio nd radar.
29. Locate forward and after auxiliary power panels, what they serve and how t cut out any equipment.
30. Locate floods for safety, negative and all fuel ballast tanks. Operate in power or hand.

31. Locate all emergency rations and fresh water.
32. Operate vapor stills. (Engineers only)
33. Know lube and fuel systems. (Engineers only)
34. Start, stop and regulate battery blowers.
35. Fire signal gun.
36. Lock stern planes.
37. Locate all collision, diving and general alarms.
38. Know ships' organization and ships' orders, and the routine for standing topside and below deck watches.
39. Know where ships' telephones are located and phraseology for talkers.
40. Understand a typical fire control problem and the necessary steps required from sighting a ship to sinking it. (Gunners torpedomen and fire controlmen only)
41. Know how to flood and sprinkle the magazine.
42. Operate all radio, radar and sound gear. (Radiomen only)
43. Understand why there is a sternplane-capstan switch in after torpedo room.
44. What is a vent riser, a flood valve, a flood and drain valve and a drain valve? How do the main vents operate?
45. What are the functions of the regulator valves on main ballast tank?
46. Understand purpose of emergency vents and how 10# and 600# air get to the main ballast tanks.
47. Know use of all valves on H.P. and 600# manifalds.
48. Operate low pressure blower.
49. Hve a brief understanding of the following: Locate these on board.
    A "B" end motor.
    An "A" end pump.
    A centrifugal pump.
    A gear type positive displacement pump.
    A screw type pump.
    A reciprocating pump.
    A lobe type pump.
50. Know on which side of the ship to find air, oil, water and hydraulic lines.

USS Toro (SS422) Rescued Airmen (9)

First Patrol – 04-24-45 thru **06-19-45** - Area 7, Bungo Suido

05-23-45, B-29 Super Fortress (Long Winded Avenger) 9th Bomber Group, 99th Squadron

1. Sgt. Robert C. Canova, USAAF, Left Gunner, 421053346
2. Pvt. 1c Charles W. Smith, USAAF, Rear Gunner 36841475
3. Staff Sgt. Howard E. Stein, USAAF, Radar Operator, 36898537
   Sgt. Howard A Fielder, USAAF, Tail Gunner, drowning witnessed

Second Patrol – 07-14-45 thru **08-20-45** - Area 6, Kii Suido

07-25-45, HMS Implacable Aircraft Carrier (RPG) Bomber Aircraft

4. Sub Lt (A) A.R. Wisdel, RNVR
5. Lt. l. A. Weus, RNVR
6. Sub. Lt. P.B.D. Wise, RNVR

07-30-45

7. 1st Lt. Lee Quarterman Jr., USAAF, Pilot, P-51 MUSTANG 0-415835

08-08-45

8. 1st Lt. Paul E. Schurr, USAAF, Pilot, 0-767402
9. Major Paul R. Wignell, USAAF, Pilot, 0-409786

About the Author

Mark H. Van Auken, originally from Elyria, Ohio, received a Bachelor of Business Administration degree from Ohio University, Athens, Ohio. While studying at OU, he was a member of the 110-member marching band known then as the Marching Men of Ohio.

He is retired from a 30-year career in banking where he was a vice president of a local bank.

He is a founding board member of the USS Indianapolis Museum, located within the Indiana War Memorial, where he held the position of Corporate Secretary.

He lives with his wife of 34 years, Sharon Van Auken, in Indianapolis, Indiana. They are the parents of Maria and Nicholas Van Auken.